LIONEL

LIONEL

LOUIS MARLIO DE L'INSTITUT

UNIFORM PRESS

First published in 1946 in French with a Preface by Louis Marlio

First published in an English translation in 2013 by
Uniform Press, an imprint of Unicorn Press Ltd
66 Charlotte Street
London W1T 4QE

www.unicornpress.org

ISBN 978 1 906509 23 1

Also available as an e-book:

e-pub ISBN 978 1906509 75 0
e-mobi ISBN 978 1906509 76 7

Designed by Camilla Fellas
Printed in the United Kingdom

Contents

MOTHER, FATHER, LIONEL, GÉRARD AND CLAUDE c. 1932

Foreword

THIS BOOK WAS FIRST PUBLISHED in French in 1946 by our stepfather Louis Marlio, a leading French Industrialist as well as a member of l'Institut de France, a branch of l'Académie Française. His purpose was to honour the memory of our brother Lionel, killed in action just two years earlier in November, 1944.

The reader must keep in mind that he wrote the preface very soon after the Second World War—a time when the scars of that devastating conflict were still fresh.

Gérard Mosséri-Marlio
Claude Mosséri-Marlio
2013

Acknowledgements

MANY PEOPLE HAVE HELPED the editor and publisher of this book with translation of the letters and with advice. Our thanks to all, especially A. Dumont, Sarah Patey of Le Mot Juste, Georgia de Chamberet of Bookblast, Ann Wadham, Danielle Thorn and David Evans.

MOTHER AND STEPFATHER, LOUIS MARLIO, c. 1936

Preface

IT WAS SHORTLY AFTER the French Armistice, June 22, 1940, that my stepson Lionel Mosséri, at the age of nineteen, volunteered as a private in the King's Royal Rifle Corps. Three years later he had risen to the rank of captain in a parachute regiment. Then, at his own request, he transferred to the French army as a second lieutenant in the 1st Commando Unit.

Lionel fell on 25 November, 1944 as he led a French detachment into Masevaux, the first city in Upper Alsace to be freed from German Occupation. He was twenty-three.

During his period of armed service, he wrote many letters. I have a number of reasons for publishing them. First, I wish to pay due honour to his memory. At a time when many wonder about the future of France, it seems that a country able to produce young men of such a calibre as Lionel, is entitled to be optimistic about its future. It is also a stark reminder to those who survived the carnage of the Second World War, of the debt they owe to those who did not—a debt which can only be repaid by efforts designed to bring about the political and social reforms needed to achieve the lasting peace for which they sacrificed their lives. In publishing this book, I am mindful not only of Lionel, but his comrades who also fell and are remembered with him.

The letters he left with us are sufficiently thought provoking and well written to justify their publication. I was asked by the publisher to supply a few pages to introduce Lionel to the reader, and describe the environment in which he was writing. I have done this only to enable the reader better to understand and appreciate the letters, and elucidate the events to which he often makes only passing allusion. It is important to point out that because of torpedo attacks, and frequent troop repositioning, half the correspondence has been lost. And of course it must also be remembered that in compliance with the strict rules governing specific squadrons and commandos, full details of the operations in which he took part were never given. A description of the context is therefore necessary if the reader is to appreciate and understand these letters, which are brimming with ideas, enthusiasm and good will. I have tried to do this, though I doubt I have fully succeeded.

The operations in which he took part were secret, and carried out in small units that were often altered and redeployed, so the information I have from the British army is limited. Enquiries to the French army were more fruitful, as he only served in one corps. The best source of information has been the personal accounts of his army comrades—those who saw him in action and his close friends, to whom he unburdened himself when secrecy was no longer needed.

His letters were not intended for publication. I present them here as they were written, simply omitting those that are of interest only to close friends and family. Lionel wrote English as well as he wrote French—perhaps even better. About ten of his letters were written in English.[1]

In bringing Lionel's letters to the public, I have tried to avoid romanticising his life in any way. My main concern has been to show the truth about his short yet remarkable career. It has been a challenge to leave to one side the tremendous affection I had for him, and the bonds of common thought that led me to promise him that after the war he would share in the intellectual work I envisaged.

---

[1] Translator's note: these were translated for the French edition, but the originals are not available. They have therefore been re-translated into English here.

This is not my book, but his. I trust the reader will find it as interesting to read as I have found it moving to put together. The subject matter of the book is the four-year period of Lionel's war as it is described in his letters and in the memories and personal reminiscences I have been able to assemble. To enable the reader better to understand his words and his actions, this biography will start with a brief portrait of the hero of this book, showing how his personality emerged between childhood and manhood.

**

A child has no history. Lionel's childhood and adolescence were free of major drama so is there no need for a lengthy description. This is just a brief summary of the key stages in his story, so we can see the evolution from child—to adolescent—to the man he became. Lionel's father, Jacques Mosséri, was a banker in Cairo, and belonged to an old Jewish Portuguese family, which immigrated to Livorno during the Inquisition and then settled in Egypt in the early 19th century.

He grew up in a villa full of flowers and sunshine. The house was welcoming and happy, and friends were entertained in a library that held manuscripts, carefully stored, dating back to Ptolemaic times. Several times a year, in the evenings, the great hall would fill with guests whom Lionel's parents had invited to hear artists visiting Cairo. Lionel, a handsome child with dark curls, dressed in a black velvet suit with a lace collar, would bow to greet the grand ladies. Arab servants, most of whom had been with the family for many years, would treat the young master with deference. This life of apparent ease was his during those early years.

Up to the age of eleven, he was educated in French, and then for two years he attended the Italian school to learn Italian. His father died in 1934. Lionel was thirteen. In keeping with the tradition of his father's family, he left Egypt to attend Gresham's, an English public school which had modern ideas in spite of its long history. He stayed on for a year after his final exams to study literature and history, and won a place at Balliol College, Oxford.

The ominous clouds of political gloom were however, gathering over Europe. Lionel wished to strengthen his ties with France, to which he felt so drawn.

In the spring of 1939 he acquired French nationality, which he had requested, and settled in Paris, hoping to take his baccalauréat two months later. Given that he had never studied in France, friends were sceptical that he would pass, but with great determination he gained a 'Mention bien', (honours), a considerably higher achievement.

It was in September of that year that war was declared. With his Mother's agreement, Lionel decided to defer his place at Oxford, stay in France, and enlist as soon as he was nineteen. He applied for officer training courses in Tours and Paris, but was told he was too young, and that there was no shortage of officers. Not willing to take 'no' for an answer, he went back to the recruitment centres, sought interviews, and laid siege to the colonel, who told me, 'I've never come across such determination.'

Lionel also took advantage of this last year of waiting to study at the Paris law faculty and at Sciences Politiques,[2] where he was fascinated by the intellectual and moral atmosphere. There, he developed a keen appetite for economics, politics

[2] The very selective faculty of political science at the university of Paris, which has traditionally educated the political and diplomatic elite.

and social studies, and was able to sharpen his thinking considerably while still finding time for sports and cultural activities, going to the theatre and concerts. He was particularly drawn by the intellectual rapport with his teachers, alongside whom he hoped to work some day.

I recall his enthusiasm and almost childish pride when asked to take part, as translator, in a symposium I organised with a few friends to discuss with Walter Lippmann the ideas he published in his challenging book *The Good Society* (translated into French as *La Cité libre*). This energetic and intelligent defence of liberalism was published at the same time as my own work developing a similar thesis, *Le Sort du Capitalisme* (*The Fate of Capitalism*). About twenty economists from a wide range of countries took part in the compelling discussions, which lasted three or four days. The participants included Robbins, Cunliffe, Hayek, Rappard, Ropke, Beveridge, Jacques Rueff, Louis Baudin, Von Mises and Louis Rougier. They all condemned the doctrines of state control and autarky that were poisoning economic life and, at the same time, bringing political disaster. All of this was fascinating to the young translator who, eyes fixed on the speaker, seemed to be experiencing the seeds of a passion, a sense of mission even. Lionel had found his way. The 'phoney war' continued until the French front collapsed and Hitler overran the country. The life that had opened up before Lionel was cut short, forcing him to abandon his library research, stimulating discussions and lectures. Long walks in the streets of old Paris and afternoons spent at the Théâtre Français would become a thing of the past. His childhood was over. Lionel the soldier was born.

**

Throughout this period, described above in the briefest of terms, the events themselves were of minor significance. It is far more interesting to record the small incidents, the words, the remarks that reveal character and give glimpses of the boy blooming into adulthood, complete with both good and bad traits; consistencies and inconsistencies. Education can give polish, but it does not change the basic person.

From his earliest childhood, Lionel was undisciplined, forceful and a fighter. During one musical evening at home, the audience, whose full attention was on a great violinist's performance, was abruptly interrupted by loud screams: Lionel tumbled down the stairs into the main hall together with his nurse. On another occasion, when he was confined to his room as a punishment, he escaped out of the window and let himself down from the third floor using a narrow gutter-pipe. At the Italian school, he was the lead mischief-maker. After a lively discussion between groups of boys labelling themselves fascists and antifascists, he broke the teeth of the boy leading the 'Mussolini' group. In the skirmish that followed, Lionel was knocked out. The headmaster visited Mr Jacques Mosséri the next day and asked him to take his son out of the school, as this one boy was causing more trouble than all the other children put together. In 1936, at Gresham's, when the Nazis occupied the left bank of the Rhine, fellow pupils criticised the imperialist attitude of the French, who appeared to threaten world peace and yet seemed incapable of sustaining a war of their own against Germany. The discussion became heated. Lionel—considered French because of his French mother—

became angry. He suggested settling the matter in single combat, and in the ensuing wrestling match, his opponent's arm was dislocated. 'There were times,' wrote Mr Newell, his headmaster at Gresham's, 'when he would try the patience of a saint.' He thrived on confrontation.

Another noticeable characteristic was a clear need to be in charge and to shine—something which can turn a child into a hero or a conceited fool. His friends nicknamed him 'Lionel the Magnificent'. At the Swiss children's home called 'Red Riding Hood', where he spent several months, the matron remarked that he would have let himself be killed if it got him noticed. He wanted to be first at everything. When he was five, at Evian, Maréchal Joffre, who enjoyed watching the pretty child with dark eyes, who was fidgeting about and being noisy, noticed him and asked, 'what do you want to do when you grow up?' Quick as a flash, the child answered, 'I shall be Maréchal de France, like you.' He loved sport, and especially riding. One day, he was thrown from his horse. He got straight back into the saddle, and when his mother praised him for being so brave he replied, 'I'm furious, because I didn't control my horse.'

It was not enough for Lionel simply to win—he had also to persuade. He was a natural-born debater. One day, after a long-drawn-out discussion with his mother, on some trivial matter, he obstinately refused to acknowledge that he might be wrong. His mother, finally losing patience said, 'that's enough argument!' Lionel answered with a smile, 'I'm not arguing, I'm pleading my case.'

Even as a very young child he enjoyed speaking in public. Once, during a school break at the Red Riding Hood, the matron noticed that, unusually, all the boys had gathered behind the house. Slightly concerned, she went to investigate, and there was Lionel, standing on an orange box, his hair a mess, gesticulating and haranguing his friends who were hanging on his every word, all agog. He craved success, and despised failure. Once, at Gresham's, he was reprimanded for some minor offence such as lateness, or untidiness. His punishment was to pick ten thousand daisies in the school grounds and arrange them in stacks of fifty. He would have preferred a more severe punishment to this, as he was humiliated in front of his school-friends.

The death of his father instilled in Lionel an increased sense of responsibility – a necessary counterbalance to authority. This first came to light within the family. 'I'm the eldest,' he said to his brother Gérard one day, 'I'll inherit from Father, but don't worry, I will always look after you.'

This sense of personal responsibility was expressed all through his life. He never sought to burden others with the consequences of his actions or his mistakes. He demanded much of himself, and considered complaining to be a sign of weakness. He had been a cherished and spoilt child, so it came as a drastic shock to find himself suddenly in an English public school where discipline among the younger boys can be harsh because it is meted out by older boys. He was an outsider in terms of race, culture and tradition, and was constantly at odds with both the temperament and habits of his schoolmates. For several years he kept quiet, especially to his mother, about his unpopularity.

He loved to spend generously on others as well as on himself. But he was not interested in money as such. When he was about to enlist, his mother sought to make him aware of his

inheritance from his father. Lionel, however, made it clear that
he found the subject extremely boring, and in the end said,
'Mother, let's talk about something else.'

The traits that we have observed so far are decidedly
masculine, and he certainly seemed well prepared to embark
on a life of action and leadership. Yet there was also a softer
side to Lionel. While it is true he was fearless in close combat,
almost welcoming it in fact, yet paradoxically, right up to
the age of sixteen, he harboured an irrational fear of ghosts.
He was compassionate towards suffering animals. He craved
affection. And, as demonstrated by his letters, he clearly
adored his Mother. When he was three, he told her, 'I love
you as much as there is water in the ocean.' With girls, he was
gentle, reserved even, preferring conversation and poetry to
taking them to a bar or a nightclub.

The letters show how four years of war took this complex
child and made him an inspiration to men on the battlefield,
as well as a potential leader in the political and social battles
of the future. Year by year, these letters trace how swiftly he
grew in maturity.

**

The letters of Lionel Mosséri are written by a soldier, a
son, and a democratic Frenchman who was both liberal and
optimistic.

He was a model soldier. I will outline briefly his military
career. He was in the British army for two years, as a cadet and
a non-commissioned officer. During this time he underwent
an intensive and varied training, including that of commando.
He then spent a year learning the skills of command as a first

lieutenant in armoured brigades in England and Africa. The last eight months were spent, first as lieutenant, then as captain in a specialised regiment in Italy and Yugoslavia, and finally, at his own request, as second lieutenant in the 1st Group of French Commandos in France in the Alsace campaign. During those final eight months he accumulated highly prized citations and medals in both armies until the day he fell during the liberation of Masevaux. During his three years of training and practice, never once did he complain that the regime was harsh and the military discipline demanding. He knew it was necessary.

From the start, he fully appreciated the profound changes in military practice between the First and Second World Wars. In 1914, war was waged using large, centralised military units, so that ordinary soldiers, as well as junior and even senior officers had little to do other than obey the orders coming from above and prepared long in advance.

In 1939, warfare required a high level of initiative and intelligence, and had an increasing tendency to require more hand to hand combat between ever smaller units under the direct command of junior officers.'[3]

He knew that a soldier's main asset was his body, which had to be maintained in top condition through dedicated physical exercise. Lionel neither smoked nor drank, and voluntarily chose not to participate in some of the luxuries of an easier life. He would avoid a laden tea-table, or too close a friendship, as he felt such indulgences would likely soften the will of a soldier and an officer and thus detract from the sole focus he should have and only object: victory. In the summer of 1943, he shared some of his dreams of the future with a young lady,

[3] Letter, 10 September, 1942.

but stopped short of making any definite commitment to her. Is it enough that a young officer need simply be a healthy male and a fine human specimen who lives a Spartan life meeting all physical challenges? For Lionel it was not. He was equally determined to achieve a high academic level of education. His thinking was twofold: it would equip him, during his time off, to avoid the depression that boredom can so easily bring, and in action, it would equip him with judgment, quick thought, and the power of decision so essential to three-dimensional mechanical warfare. In modern battle, situations evolve before your very eyes, and an officer has very little time, sometimes only a split second, to assess the situation before making his decision which, whether right or wrong, will be irrevocable.

Lionel also knew that in a unit designed to execute sudden attacks, which could be both daring and dangerous, the success of any operation depends above all on the cohesion of the group, on good communication between officer and men, and the complete confidence of the men in their leader. The officer must be understood, instantaneously. During an attack or secret operation, ranks, decorations and stripes count for nothing. The team is a single unit, taking its lead from the commanding officer's slightest gesture, and expecting from him, instant decisions.

To be in such a position of leadership, one has to warrant it. This was Lionel's goal and he worked towards achieving it. 'His men', he wrote on the day he was commissioned, 'make up a splendid unit: I hope they will respect and trust me.'[4] And he was immediately conscious of his responsibility for them: an officer's first duty is to ensure that the lives of his men are as safe as possible, and once the operational targets are met,

[4] Letter, 12 January, 1943.

to bring home as many of them as possible. He has to watch over them; ensure their physical wellbeing; ensure on arrival at any billet that they are housed and fed; check, as soon as he has finished dinner in the mess, that all is in order for the night; provide entertainment and games for times of rest; provide help and counsel in personal and family difficulties, such as the birth of a baby, or the arrival of an anonymous letter; these, Lionel felt were his duties commanding a platoon. He was 'adored by his men'[5] and when he fell, his sergeant, Trompette, expressed his emotion and his deep sense of loss in these sober words: 'In losing him, I've lost everything.'

In battle, he claimed the most difficult tasks for himself, always wanting to be at the forefront, and he felt cheated if he didn't take the most dangerous position.[6] One of his men wrote to us, 'Often, when I think of the late Lionel I get lost in thought. I shall never forget brave Lieutenant Mosséri.'[7] Lionel knew the secret techniques used by the Japanese and the American Indians to overcome an armed opponent. He had witnessed such terrible atrocities committed by the Germans in Yugoslavia that he had developed a personal hatred towards them, and had sworn to kill as many as possible by his own hand and with a dagger.

It is not for me to laud his military prowess. His promotion, so quickly achieved, the stripes he earned, and extracts of letters from his commanding officers and fighting comrades will make the point more eloquently than I can.[8]

To those who knew the quarrelsome and mercurial small child, it seemed obvious that Lionel would become a magnificent soldier. But it may have been more surprising to those who remembered the ill-disciplined schoolboy and his

[5] Letter from Lieutenant-Colonel Vallon, 12 January, 1945
[6] Note from Captain Ruais.
[7] Letter from Sergeant Trompette, 21 January, 1946.
[8] See the Appendix.

adherence to the Oxford Movement[9] and its pacifist doctrines.

It does indeed seem at first sight that the war gave rise to a complete metamorphosis in Lionel. Is it possible to speak of pacifism in relation to an officer with such a brilliant war record? Is it possible to speak of ill discipline in relation to a soldier who draws on his acceptance of military service in shaping the way he exercises his command? He had an unquestioning admiration for his commanding officers, for their bravery and intelligence; he fully respected the superlative training methods used by Alexander and Montgomery to prepare the British army, fully expecting them to deliver an early victory; he later praised the boldness and enthusiasm of his French commando comrades.

He was not affected by that pervasive tendency to question and criticise any orders from superiors. He may sometimes have had a gentle dig at the very strict etiquette governing British officers, but he was always quick to point out that this formalism in no way undermined the very close relationship between officers and men in manoeuvres and on the battlefield.

Life in barracks or in camp was not always to his taste, but he wrote philosophically 'I don't know why everything conspires to build my character.'[10]

It would be too simplistic to assume that the declaration of war had dispelled, as though by magic, his ill discipline and pacifism. These two character traits remained, if temporarily set aside. Lionel accepted the necessity of war. For him it had to be as demanding and tough as possible, not because he liked war, but because this hateful process seemed to him the only way to overcome the scourge of Hitler as well as ensuring the political and social peace of which he dreamed. He killed so that

[9] The Oxford Group Movement, later MRA (Moral Re-Armament)
[10] Letter, 19 October, 1941.

others would not have to. The same phrases recur throughout his military life.

What mattered above all was clearly to proclaim the aims of the war, and then the nature of the political and societal life that would follow it. Anyone who fights without knowing why was to him despicable. Anyone who hoped to go home after the fighting without expecting to work for the dividends of peace was reprehensible. Anyone who killed without having a worthy reason was an assassin.

Lionel was waging war, but war was not his life but a phase between the illusions and naivety of his youth and of his life as a man, when he planned to share with others his ideals of justice and freedom, and to help create, for the benefit of all, the democratic civilisation that modern scientific progress is making possible.

As for the disciplined soldier, he did not sacrifice his independence of thought. As soon as victory was won, he was prepared to fight on for the victory of his ideas, as he fought during the war to overcome his enemy. In spite of everything, he remained a revolutionary, rebelling against all compromise, and against any apathy that might generate future wars. After the war, he would become a political leader and lead the fight for a truly democratic and liberal world, an ideal that we both shared.

**

His letters not only convey his ideas on military matters but also, the deep affection he had for his family. This part of his writing is truly charming. Two letters are addressed to friends; three to the young lady of whom he had grown fond in 1943;

and all the others to his mother. It would be difficult to find any letters from a son to his mother that showed more affection and trust. He thinks of her at all times. They are essentially the letters of a son to his mother.

The letters came erratically, and in both senses nearly half of them didn't reach their destination. 'Quite a number of my friends are engaged, and yet it's the letters from their mothers that they await with the greatest impatience; you can imagine how keenly I wait to hear from mine, since I'm not even engaged!'[11]

He had not seen his mother since she had left for America in the summer of 1940, so he explored with her all the different ways in which they could be in touch. He would telephone her when he was on leave, and once even tried to board a bomber to come and spend two or three days in Washington. His hopes were dashed, as strict military discipline forbade this. As time passed, he increasingly felt—and suffered from—the pain of separation. On 9 November, 1943, he telegraphed, 'All is well, but I'm so miserable that I have been so far from you for such a long time. I dream of crossing the Atlantic, even if I have to swim it, to bring to you my warmest wishes.' A few weeks later he wrote, 'At Christmas, I suddenly had a fierce longing to leave camp, steal an aeroplane, and fly over to join you.'[12]

To comfort himself and his mother for the irregular nature of their correspondence, he wrote, 'Even though we are so far apart, I both feel and know that there are ways we communicate that are more lasting and more effective than pen and paper. I feel that, for things that really matter, neither you nor I have any need to write them down.'[13] This is no literary platitude. I am not naturally inclined to believe in the supernatural, but it

[11] Letter, 2 June, 1941.
[12] Letter, 1 January, 1944.
[13] Letter, 3 April, 1941.

did seem that every time Lionel was in any danger, or in poor health, his mother seemed to know it before she was told. I will dwell on only two examples.

One winter Sunday, returning home from a concert, his mother, who was not normally anxious, said to me, 'I don't know why, but I'm worried about Lionel, and I'm going to call him.' Half an hour later she got through to the head of the college where he was studying, who told him that Lionel couldn't come to the phone as he had broken his arm playing football.

On 25 November, 1944, the day Lionel was killed, his mother said to me, 'Something has happened; in the night, I heard one of my sons saying to me: Mother, Mother, come quickly.' She was so struck by this that she spoke about it to several other people that very day.

In his letters to his mother, Lionel showed much gratitude to her for the education she had given him. He had one major setback when training as an officer which he minded all the more because he feared his mother would be disappointed. And when he did become an officer, it was to her that he very movingly expressed his commitment to his duty: 'If ever, when I am hungry, cold, in pain, or fearful; if at that moment I continue in spite of everything to do my duty, it will probably be because I remember having written this letter and am justified in doing so.'[14]

One of his female friends[15] said that for him his mother was always 'the Madonna.' At one point, he writes of his own childhood memories. 'I remember one night when I was very small: you were so beautiful, wearing an evening gown, looking like a fairy or a queen, I'm not sure which, but you

[14] Letter, 4 December, 1942.
[15] Mademoiselle Linette Terré.

were quite certainly my very own mother, standing by my
bed and promising to come back soon. Now it's my turn to
make that promise.'[16] He was keen to reassure his mother
about the dangers he would encounter. 'My tailor has made
me a superb uniform, and I promise you'll see me wearing it
without any holes or tears.'[17] And his very last letter ended,
'We have reached the last hundred metres. I shall finish the
race unhurt.'[18]

Lionel's letters to his mother show a surprising modesty.
He rarely talks of what he has done himself, of his rank or
of any stripes gained. It was only by chance that his mother
found a letter amongst his papers from which she learned that
at twenty-two, he had been made captain in a special regiment
of the British Army. She showed the First Secretary at the
British Embassy in Washington two medals pinned to his
uniform, and that was how she found out that one of them
was one of the highest British decorations, the Distinguished
Service Order, rarely given to a young officer. Why was he so
covert about his achievements?

In part, he was respecting the secrecy of the secret missions
in which he was engaged, but above all he did not wish to boast.
His friend Linette wrote to us on 25 February, 1945, 'He was
so wonderful, your son, several times he said to me with great
modesty, "Please can you tell Mother what I've done—you
see, I can't tell her about it".'

In nearly every letter, he wrote about his two brothers.
Lionel was not worried about the younger one, Claude, who
was very like him in many ways. He thought he would have
a straightforward life. 'The lights will always be green for
him,' and elsewhere, 'Just make sure he learns how to have

[16] Letter, 1 January, 1944.
[17] Letter, 4 December, 1942.
[18] Letter, 15 October, 1944.

fun.' The older one, Gérard, was only four years his junior. As he approached the age when he would have to enlist, Lionel's worries intensified. He shared his concerns with his mother. Would Gérard serve, as he had done, in the British Army, even though he was a French citizen, or would he join the French army? Lionel invariably concluded that the best thing for Gerard would be for him to continue with his university studies.[19] He gives excellent reasons for this opinion, but does not give the main one. He feels he is taking the risks and – for the sake of both his mother and his brother—he wishes to remain the only one to do so. If Gérard could delay enlisting for a few months, he would avoid being sent to the front before the end of the war.

Gérard, however, did not follow this advice and enlisted at eighteen in the French naval air force. Lionel wrote him a letter almost paternal in tone, giving him advice arising out of his own experience and wishing him 'Good luck and good hunting.'[20]

**

Lionel Mosséri wrote above all as a Frenchman. He was French through and through. Six months after Munich, and two months after the invasion of Czechoslovakia, he applied for French nationality so that, as soon as he was old enough, he would to be able to fight for France in the inevitably approaching war. It was for the sake of France that immediately after the occupation in 1940 he asked, although French, to serve in the British Army, which alone was continuing to fight the German tyrant. And it was 'For the honour of serving as second lieutenant in the French commandos'[21] that he gave

[19] Letters, 10 September, 1942, 2 June, 1943, 20 October, 1943, 22 December, 1943 and April, 1944
[20] Letter end of May, 1944.

up the rank of captain in a specialised regiment of the British Army in order to commit himself more fully and immediately to the fight for France. And it was for France that he fell at the liberation of Masevaux.

Lionel chose to be French, and his heart was fully French. He had been educated in England, and had a profound admiration for that great country, its leaders, its teachers, its secular structure, the way in which progress was tempered by tradition, the importance of etiquette and of fair play, its wonderful sense of unity and of the greatness of Empire, its respect for the freedom both of individuals and of the nation. But it was France that he loved, and he loved to remember the year he spent in France in 1939–40. He had felt completely at home in Paris, studying law and at Sciences Politiques, and that was where he made his greatest friendships. It was not a rational decision to give up his English military career in order to join the French army. He was leaving an army that was wonderfully well run and equipped, in which he was already known, and in which his rank gave him a greater role. He was embracing a lower rank in an army short of materials and resources yet which was being rebuilt. But this did not matter to Lionel. He had met fellow Frenchmen, all volunteers, who had risked their lives and perhaps endangered the safety of their mothers or wives by escaping from France; these Frenchmen spoke of freeing France, of taking revenge on the Germans, of marching on Berlin. They were led by officers who had proved their worth in very difficult conditions.

Lionel recognised in them the patriotism that had inspired the poorly-equipped volunteers of Valmy and Jemmapes who repelled the invaders in 1792. He saw the same spark. It was

[21] Army order no. 802.

with these men that Lionel wished to finish fighting the war. Colonel Gambiez wrote, 'he was like a cherished child... he was very specially ours.'[22] A few weeks after he died, I was discussing Lionel's impulsive move with Colonel Benson, the Military Attaché at the British Embassy in Washington. I wondered whether Benson had been surprised at what was an arguably unreasonable chivalric gesture. 'Not at all,' replied Benson, putting his hands to his chest, 'It just proves that he had something here.'

What Lionel loved about France was its culture and its spirit. He loved the logic of the law, the precision of the language, the wonder of its words; he loved its poetry, and the harmony and simplicity of the combined whole.

Above all, Lionel loved French ideas—those ideas that have made French ideology great and have carried the spirit of France around the world. He was a Frenchman of the Revolution: when he heard Churchill's great Atlantic Charter speech, he felt he was listening to the Declaration of the Rights of Man. 'I felt,' he wrote, 'That this might be the most important moment of my life... I was suddenly overcome with gratitude and whispered, "Thank you!"'[23]

In fighting for France, he was not merely hoping to liberate all of France but, like the volunteers in 1793, he was fighting to ensure that everywhere, independence and human rights could be enjoyed by all.

Lionel was a democrat. In the United States, he had seen the wonders that a great democracy can achieve through an alert public with an informed and independent press. He realised that in a true democracy, one could not hope that all should live in a similar manner, but one could aim to give

---

[22] The letter of Colonel Gambiez, who led Lionel's brigade, is in the Appendix.
[23] Letter, 22 March, 1943.

everyone the same opportunities, so everyone could achieve the best they could according to their aptitudes, whether inherited or acquired, and their commitment to hard work. He knew that communism was a mere caricature of democracy. It combined harsh political dictatorship and bureaucratic exploitation of people through extreme capitalist measures that must be anathema to any democracy. And he knew too that dictatorship would lead to war.

Lionel was my student. He was an unabashed liberal and thought it far better to leave man free to decide his own actions, rather than have him enslaved or directed by a state. The overdevelopment of state structures is surely one of the great ills of the modern world.

He had seen in America that a liberal system, well understood and well used, was able to deliver increasing material comfort to the people, more free time and better ways to use it, and that this did not mean people had to abdicate their rights and freedom to a higher authority that might be brutal, incompetent and overwhelming.

He knew that economic liberalism could not exist only within one country, but needed international exchange and cooperation if it were to flourish, keep prices low, and ensure future peace.

And he also knew that one should not confuse patriotism, which welcomes and tolerates, with isolationism, which is a hateful caricature of patriotism. In him lived again the great revolutionaries who promised peace to the world.

**

I will not have done justice to Lionel until I depict one final aspect of his personality. Although he was by nature somewhat nervous, Lionel was thoroughly and intentionally optimistic. As far as the war was concerned, he was completely confident that it would turn out right. 'The day will come—as sure as the sun rises—when it will be our turn to land on the beaches. I pity those who will face one of our bayonet charges.'[24] 'Nothing can break the combined strength of English spirit and American equipment.'[25] 'Today, the British Army is the best in the world: when our turn comes... then neither I nor anyone else will need to talk.'[26] 'The British Army has been training furiously... for two years, and has not yet shown its full potential: when the moment comes, the Germans are going to cop it!'[27] When he transferred into the French army, he wrote, 'This is an elite unit... The army of De Lattre de Tassigny is already magnificent, and I really hope that we shall soon be in the heart of Germany, ahead of the other Allied forces.'[28]

His optimism was not limited to military operations. The war made no sense to him if it was not to bring about a better life for people afterwards. It seemed to him that the signs had never been more promising. 'For the first time,' he wrote, 'It will be possible to set up a democratic government as Rousseau intended it. We shall be able to abolish classes through the levelling effect of education, and we shall be able to meet the economic needs of people and even give them some leisure time.'[29] The same optimism is to be found in a wonderful letter describing his idea of an economic system:[30] 'In the end, any economic or political doctrine is based either on optimism and trust or on pessimism and mistrust. Myself, I prefer trust.' His thought flowed from this principled position. A pessimist

[24] Letter, 3 April, 1941.
[25] Letter, 2 June, 1941.
[26] Letter, 2 June, 1941.
[27] Letter, 15 July, 1943.

[28] Letter, 15 October, 1944.
[29] Letter, April, 1944.
[30] Letter, 26 July, 1944.

would require the state to take the place of a man who was dangerous or incapacitated, but Lionel advocated the highest level of individual freedom. In many of his letters, Lionel expressed confidence in the future; however a few of them betray a streak of bitterness and pessimism. I do not mean those in which he vents his impatience to gain promotion or to engage in a challenging mission. These are small frustrations which vanish like dew in the morning.

But during his last few months a growing anxiety and discouragement are perceptible. He is still confident that peace can be achieved and that the world of the future can be better organised. His pessimism, he writes, is because nations and their leaders seem not to be choosing the right road, or indeed seem not to be aware of a huge task awaiting them once victory is won. In two of his letters it seems that his optimism is somewhat shaken;[31] he fears that the commitment and heroism displayed during the war may have been for nothing, and that the civilised world may have suffered the pain inflicted by the Nazis in vain.

I should add that this anxiety did not last and his last letter is full of confidence.[32] 'Maybe you will remember', he wrote, 'That in one of my letters I tried to describe the team spirit in which, with my men, I would like to fight the good fight. Well, I have finally found those men and that spirit; I am happy— happier than I have been for a long time.'

**

I have tried to describe and analyse a complex and varied personality; sometimes even paradoxical. So, what is the general picture of Lionel that emerges from his correspondence? He

[31] Letters, 22 December, 1943 and 10 April, 1944.
[32] Letter, 26 July, 1944.

was an idealist, but in no way a visionary. Asceticism held no attractions for him, and he enjoyed and valued the good things of this world. He had dedicated his life to the study of economics. He thought scientific progress would enable human progress.

But he also knew that for individuals, societies and for the world, a materialistic approach to life could lead only to failure. He also knew that technical progress—which favours the use of force and which, used injudiciously, can bring chaos—could lead men astray and cause world conflict in the absence of a parallel development of justice and generosity.

His love of France was not only because he found there both taste and culture. The leaders of the 1789 revolution had brought freedom to the world and offered each person the opportunity to develop his full potential. Yet they had also introduced the concepts of equality and brotherhood as correctives, so that peace could be maintained between the different levels of society and nations.

He loved the French spirit of balance between individual liberty and social justice, between patriotism and the spirit of international collaboration. He thought, as I do, that these ideas and principles gave rise to the glory of France in the past and will give birth to a glorious French renaissance in the future.

Had he lived, I sometimes wonder if Lionel would have recognised the country I have just described in the France we know today. Its defects are all too obvious; and in the eighteen months since the liberation, they became more rather than less marked. Did we see the true face of France during this period? What does France look like at the end of 1945? An arbitrary executive authority which is powerless; a

Press lacking information and paper; an electorate weary and depressed by material shortages and still infected by Nazi propaganda. Young people are enthusiastic, but seem unsure of democracy, and relegate freedom to a secondary position. The political parties all conspire to overthrow the institutions of the third Republic rather than to put them right; the country as a whole seems not to recognise the debt it owes to a regime that brought it back from the brink of disaster in 1870, and for seventy years has fostered greater magnificence and prosperity in the intellectual field—both in science and in the arts—as well as in the colonies, industry and finance, than the country experienced under Louis XIV or during the brief apotheosis of Napoleon I.

The country seems inclined to withdraw, nursing its bruised dignity, and to no longer acknowledge its position in the world. State control is on the increase, and bureaucracy is growing, but not necessarily in competence or honesty. There is a tendency to isolationism, something a rich victorious nation could possibly allow itself, but France cannot afford high prices and international isolation—today, more than ever, she needs help from other nations and to co-operate with them.

Lionel seemed to sense that things might go wrong when he said that he was sure to succeed in the France of 1940, but was not so sure of his chances in the France of tomorrow. He would find it all very painful, but would he withdraw into his tent? No. He was determined to fight for his ideas as fiercely as he fought for his country, or rather, he thought that to defend his ideas would be an even better way of fighting for his country than to fight the Germans. He was keen to engage in this battle as soon as the war was finished. 'I shall write in the journals and magazines; I shall speak in Parliament and, if necessary, in public.'

He had true leadership gifts that would have served him well in such political endeavours; he had a war record that would have given his words great authority; he had all the gifts required for a good fight. But all this was dashed by his premature death.

PART I

From the French defeat until Lionel joined the British Army

WHEN FRANCE WAS DEFEATED, Lionel left with us for Bordeaux, where the scattered remnants of the government and Parliament had taken refuge. He witnessed the most dreadful scenes and saw how terror can paralyse a great nation. As soon as there was talk of an armistice, I had decided to leave France and to continue the fight from the United States where I hoped to persuade that great democracy that it could play a major role in the armed struggle, which indeed it subsequently did.

When disaster struck France, Lionel was only eighteen. He sought immediately to join the British Army, the only remaining opponent to Germany. On 21 June, I went with him to the British Embassy. Diplomatic relations were about to be broken and the ambassador had already left. We were, however, able to see the military attaché. Lionel presented his case himself: during the First World War, his father had fought in the Palestine campaign with General Allenby and he himself had studied for six years in England. Although he was French, he wanted to serve as a soldier in the British Army.

The military attaché thanked him, but as the ambassador had already left, and he was packing up and about to head off, he was unable to give a reply. 'However,' he added, 'you're right to go to the United States with your parents. I will give you a good letter of recommendation for my colleague in Washington and I'm sure he will be able to help you enlist.' The next day, the armistice was signed, and we all left: Lionel, my wife, her younger son Claude, and I. Our journey across the border and through Spain and Portugal was challenging in places, and we arrived in New York on 15 July, 1940.

A few days later, Lionel and I went to Washington to see the British ambassador, Lord Lothian, who gave us a warm welcome. When Lionel told him about his decision, he replied after a pause, 'Young man, the war may be very short or it may be very long. Wait three months before you enlist. If the war is going well, as I hope it will, you will still have plenty of time to fight. In the meantime, go and see the military attaché, who is expecting you; he will give you all the information you need and will inform the Ministry of War in London.' Lionel followed these instructions.

He was somewhat disappointed and frustrated by the prospect of three months without work. I therefore suggested he spend the time working as my secretary. He enthusiastically agreed.

I had set myself a difficult task. I was working on my own, not in any official capacity, and my means in America were limited. I was not proposing to spread propaganda about my country, but simply to describe what I had seen and what I knew. I did not wish to tell the Americans that they should join the war—that would in any case have been illegal—but I wanted to help them see the huge challenge facing them in terms of arms production and the decisions that lay ahead.[33]

To achieve this, I only had my own friends on whom to rely. Most were industrialists belonging to the Republican

[33] I reported the results of this mission to the academy of moral and political sciences in two reports dated 8 October and 6 November 1945, during the presidency of Mr Charles-Roux, who had been Foreign Secretary at the time I had left France.

Party, so they were fundamentally isolationist in outlook. Presenting information to them in a sincere and objective way was, I thought, the most effective way forward. Any success I had would be all the more effective, since the Republican Party controlled most of the newspapers and magazines.

Lionel was most helpful to me in preparing my campaign, which was due to start with a trip lasting several months across the whole of America. There was no time to lose. I entrusted to Lionel a very time-consuming job: he was to make a list of all my contacts in industry, commerce, banking, teaching, the press and in politics; he was then to visit or telephone them, and ask for introductions to their friends. He was also to plan my itinerary, make appointments in advance and make notes of the conversations he held and the reactions of those to whom he spoke. For a young secretary, this was a major challenge. But this was not all: every evening, he was to give me a two-hour lesson in English, as mine was at the time very limited. I took him with me to all my meetings and he proved an excellent interpreter. The president of the University of Chicago, Mr R. Hutchins, a leading American academic, was very impressed. Three years later, when I was delivering a lecture at his university, he asked, 'What happened to that son of yours who spoke the best English I ever heard?'

I will highlight here just two important meetings to which he accompanied me. In August 1940, the Republican presidential candidate, Wendell Wilkie, was preparing his acceptance speech and had asked a dozen friends to prepare for him an economic and social policy. The meeting took place at Lennox, Massachusetts, at the home of Mr Raymond Buell. I had been invited and was to give my views. The round-table discussion lasted three days, and I could never get hold of my secretary just when I needed him most. He was so absorbed by the importance of the issues being debated that during the gaps between meetings, as well as every evening, he was involved in endless discussions with the various guests.

The following week, the National Association of Manufacturers, the largest industrial organisation of its kind in America, invited me to Hotsprings, Virginia, for its annual general meeting. For three days, they reviewed the major matters of current political and professional importance. In the last session, before the final dinner, I delivered a speech describing what had led to the French disaster, in which I particularly emphasised that mechanised war was a new phenomenon, and that the German military machine had tremendous power. Naturally, I urged my audience to see that America could have a major impact by swift, intense investment in the production of armaments. The president thanked me cordially and suggested that the session be closed.

But one of those present said, 'Before we dine, I would like to ask the young man accompanying his father about his own thoughts on the matter.' Others agreed with him, and without hesitation, in front of sixty or eighty people representing the elite of American industry, Lionel stood up. He spoke for fifteen minutes, completely unprepared, and his youthful eloquence charmed his audience. He spoke of the moral standing France had always enjoyed, and said that he was going to join the army in a few weeks, not only to liberate his country but also to fight for his ideals of freedom and societal peace both within and between countries. Mr W. R. Castle, a former Secretary of State to President Hoover, told his wife when he returned home that evening: 'Today I heard a speech by a young Frenchman; it's a real shame he is leaving the country; we need young people of his calibre here.'[34]

The three months that Lord Lothian had set him were now over, and Lionel was nineteen. I would have been glad to keep him with me until the end of my tour, but he refused and left us one very cold evening at Chicago Station. We never saw him again.

His stay in the United States had been very short, but it had made a profound impression on him. He saw America as a land that was truly democratic, enjoying both liberty and freedom of thought. He approved of the social awareness of some of the major industrialists, and noticed that although discussions on levels of pay between bosses and workmen could be heated, they never provoked class hatred, which seemed not to exist in America.

He was surprised that one of my friends, the chief executive of a major steelworks in Detroit, had started his career on the factory floor in 1920, and was very proud of where he had come from.

He was impressed by the wisdom of a New York taxi driver who had previously owned a factory with four hundred staff: he told us with a smile that he had given up his previous job and scaled down because he felt that the money made from industry was insufficient reward for all the worry and burden of responsibility.

Before he left Chicago, Lionel wrote a thank you letter to a wonderful Francophile Lady, Mrs Patch, who had made us warmly welcome in Gloucester, a lovely coastal location near Boston.

---

[34] This little incident was told to me by M.W.R. Castle himself, at a Washington dinner three years later.

Letter to Mrs Patch
Chicago, 14 October, 1940

Dear Mrs Patch,

I should have written earlier but I have been very busy these last eight days. My father has arranged his tour in such a way that we are constantly on the road. In a way, this is inevitable. America is so big, so interesting and has so much to teach us Europeans that we have had scant time to cover the distances required.

The more I see of the United States, the more I like them. I'm afraid I crossed the Atlantic with my mind full of preconceptions. I don't know why, but I imagined the typical American to be a large gentleman lacking in culture, with a loud voice and loud clothes. You gave us the most charming hospitality. You know such a lot about my country, and in such detail, that I was shamed by the mistaken impressions I had of yours.

And now, with my stepfather, I've seen wonderful factories producing unimagined riches, and dedicated businessmen working with huge commitment for the defence of their nation and motivated only by love of their country. More importantly, I've seen a likely solution to the old problems of freedom and class struggles. I visited the village of Kohler where every workman drives his own car and lives in his own house—a car and a house such that few well-off Europeans would be able to afford—and where children live a healthy peaceful life, playing on beautiful lawns and studying in wonderful buildings.

I know I mustn't let myself be carried away with wild enthusiasm at having glimpsed Plato's dream, but the fact that his vision has been realised somewhere, even though not yet everywhere, shows how much America has achieved.

When I leave for England next week, I shall have marvellous memories and a tremendous story to tell: one can still find all that is good in our modern civilisation, in terms of material wellbeing and of morality, and this present war is not being fought over the grave of a past age.

Please give my greetings to all your family, and may I thank you all for everything you did for us.

Yours sincerely,

Lionel.

From Chicago, Lionel went to stay for a few days with his aunt in New York, where something poignant happened. For the previous three months, Lionel had been thinking only of enlisting as soon as possible. At the last moment though, he suddenly felt a touch of depression, anxiety, fear even. He suddenly had a clear picture of all the dear people and places he was leaving, and was aware of the terrible things that lay ahead. He was leaving family life—he had had little enough experience of it and yet had enjoyed it so much. He was leaving his beloved mother, and a delightful young lady he had met in Chicago to whom he was strongly attracted. Ahead lay loneliness, a hostile ocean, the hard life of a military camp in a foreign country, cold, hunger, fighting; he might be wounded or—worse than death—be disabled or tortured. He was at an age when life is full of promise, and suddenly he faced doubts about willingly taking on such risks. He shared his anxiety with his aunt, and she called us the next morning to tell us how he was feeling. My wife immediately telephoned her son and told him he was under no obligation, either moral or otherwise, to anyone, and if he had doubts, he should think again. Lionel did not deny that he had indeed had some misgivings, but he said he had thought everything through during the night and he was certain he wanted to go. When he left for the army, it was not from thoughtless enthusiasm, but after making a decision with a cool head to follow his conscience and do his duty.

A few days later he went to see his two brothers who were studying at Exeter, New Hampshire, and reported to his mother on how he had found them.

New York, 28 October, 1940

Dear Mother,

I'm just back from Exeter. Claude's wild yells are still ringing in my ears and my back is still bruised from where Gérard gave me a welcoming slap.

They're both extremely well, especially Claude, whom I've never seen so lively, cheerful and full of fun. Now that he is separated from his brother, he has learned English very quickly. He speaks a lot but understands only as much as he wants. The lights will always be green for him, and life one sunny stretch.

As for Gérard, he is evidently trying very hard. His room is tidy, his books and files are kept in very good order and he has good friends. However his results aren't brilliant. First, although he is always at his very best in exams, I think he's been thrown in at the deep end and often finds himself floundering. Second, he's not good at working on his own.

He has almost as many study periods as teaching periods, and this is not helping. He really needs more guidance. He's being encouraged to discover things for himself, but he really needs more structure. He's too tempted by the amount of freedom he has: ping-pong, football and the cinema are much more fun than Latin and maths, especially when one has many good friends.

However, I think he's starting to learn how to make better use of his time, and his tutor promised me he would keep a more careful eye on him. He has a new timetable now (he's been put back one year) so he should find it easier to stay afloat. If his marks next month are disappointing, you may tell him off—he will certainly deserve it. However, right now it would probably be unfair to get angry with him.

My ship sails on Wednesday and I'm just making my last preparations. I'm leaving America with much more hope than when I left Portugal. The picture in my mind is clearer and stronger, and I feel supported by good friends and a greater level of confidence in myself.

I'm so grateful for letting me go. I know that my leaving will be hardest on you and I only hope that I can be worthy of you.

Your Lionel, who loves you.

Two days later, he boarded the ship for England, and arrived after about ten days.

His first few letters give a daily account of his deep admiration for the courage of the British population, which was fully stretched and united in its desire to resist both airborne attacks and the threat of invasion. He told us also about de Gaulle launching his movement, and about his own efforts to enlist in the British Army while retaining his French nationality. The process was complicated and slow, and he called on the help of the two men who had treated him as an adopted son during his stay in England, and whose names appear often in his letters. One is Mr Leo d'Erlanger, a friend of mine and the general manager of one of the big four private banks in London, who was incredibly kind to him, chasing up contacts and welcoming him into his home every weekend and for every leave. The other was Mr Philip Newell, a wonderful teacher who had been his headmaster at Gresham's School, where he tried to combine a modern approach and the traditional English system which is one of the strengths of the British nation.[35]

It is remarkable that two of his letters, written before he had even enlisted as a simple soldier, show that he was already concerned about clarifying the aims of the war and the conditions of the peace to come.

12 November, 1940

Dearest Mother,

As my telegram will have told you, I reached the other side of the Pond after a good crossing. The only incident of note happened as we arrived, when a gentleman protested vigorously and most eloquently, but unfortunately in vain, at the impudence of the pretty young lady from the censorship service who insisted on reading his love letters.

As soon as I arrived in London, I went to see Mr d'Erlanger. He could not have been kinder, and is now looking after me,

[35] A letter from Mr Newell describing his memories of Lionel as both school-boy and soldier is in the appendix.

which as you may well believe, is bearing fruit. He was very pleased and interested to hear the news I was able to give him of his wife.

Everyone here is focused on winning the war. The English have been buoyed up by their success in Italy and are not discouraged: this is one of the few things that the American newspapers have neither exaggerated nor got wrong. This war is bringing out the best in the British, and is ridding them of some of the prejudices and old-fashioned ways that can make them seem distant or unapproachable, sometimes even unfriendly, to those who don't know them. I'm planning to stay in London for a few days longer, as it is reasonably calm here, and then I shall go and see Mr Newell, who doesn't yet know I have arrived.

I don't have a great deal to do, but I'm not bored. I have started to read again and I'm writing about what I saw in the United States, as my ideas are clearer now. As ever, I think of you constantly with gratitude and fondness, and I hope we shall be separated for less time than anticipated.

I have a very clear picture of you in my mind, and in my imagination I am giving a big hug to you and to parrain.[36]

Lionel

London, 25 November, 1940

[36] Parrain, meaning godfather or mentor, was the familiar term Lionel used for me, and it reflected the spiritual and moral relationship that we shared.

Dearest Mother,

I have just spent a week with Mr Newell. It's been seven days of strong and at times inexplicable emotions. I've been visited by ghosts and thoughts from the past that I had consigned to a dark and dusty corner, from which they jumped out at me. Some I thought I had laid to rest, indeed discarded and almost forgotten; suddenly here they were again full of vigour.

The old school bell sounds the same it used to, and the smell of soft earth and sweat after a game of rugby is the same as I and my schoolfellows knew. Only the names have changed. The school has been transported from one side of England to the other,[37] so the beautiful forests, the fields and the wonderful buildings you will remember are all missing, but my alma mater has kept its spirit and its character in its new unpretentious home. For once, the content has mastered the form. Many of Gérard's former friends at Gresham's School asked me how he was enjoying his new life. When they heard about it, they exclaimed, 'Hope we get sent there!' And Mr Spencer, his former teacher, said, 'Send him back'. This gave rise to a lively debate about the value of American education.

Mr Newell was extremely busy, but he was most kind to me and I returned to London in good spirits.

Tell parrain that for the moment the attitude of the English towards the French seems unlikely to change much: a bit distant, but full of sympathy. This should please him at least as much as the very fond greetings I send to him, and to you and Claude.

Your Lionel.

London, 20 December, 1940.

---

[37] Gresham's was evacuated to Newquay, in Cornwall, from June 1940 to March 1944.

Dear Mother,

It's nearly New Year. When it comes I shall probably still be a student and not yet a soldier. For the first two weeks, Mr d'Erlanger thought that my problem could be solved fairly quickly, but unfortunately there are several stumbling blocks:

1. *Any Frenchman in England who wants to join the fighting is supposed to join de Gaulle.*

2. *No one is being granted British nationality while the war is on.*

It is possible they may make an exception for me and allow me to enlist, even though I'm French, because

a. *Father won several British decorations, and the War Office seemed impressed by this.*[38]

b. *De Gaulle does not yet have any structures in place for training recruits, and since I might be a useful liaison officer, they might be willing to train me in the British Army.*

As for the nationality problem that parrain was worrying about, it seems there are provisions in law and in certain commitments made by the British government. So it looks as if, sooner or later, I will be able to enlist in a way that will please both parrain and me,[39] but I will have to wait, perhaps for six weeks, according to both Mr d'Erlanger and my uncle Alexander.

Life is quite good here. Rationing is not too severe, and the bomb damage seems remarkably little, though of course in some places it is very bad.

The last few days I've been living in a new room, one that I was keen to have as I think it is the best: it's nice, as big as your bedroom was on Avenue Bugeaud, well furnished and

[38] M. Jacques Mosséri had been part of the Palestine army during the 1914 war, with Lord Allenby.

[39] That is to say, without giving up his French nationality.

cheerful; it faces south and is very peaceful so that I'm able to read a great deal. My latest discovery is an Italian economist, Antonio de Viti de Marco. His books on public finance are, in their own way, at least as good as Lippmann and Siegfried are in theirs.

How are Gérard and Claude? I wrote to them not very long ago, but I'm not expecting an answer before next year. I hope the New Year will be as happy as it can be for all of you. Much love to both you and parrain,

Lionel.

London, 1 January, 1941

Dearest Mother,

It's twilight on the first day of the year. The fog lifted gradually during the daylight hours, so that now the last rays of the sun are shining splendidly before it goes down. Symbolic, maybe? I hope so; indeed I believe so.

Last week, I wrote to you that life is continuing almost normally in London. Today, we have had one of the worst bombing raids of the war, yet I can still say the same thing: life goes on as usual. Usual, that is, because this little accountant[40] does not deem it extraordinary that he should take his turn to keep watch on a roof between three and six o'clock in the morning; because, if the buses were not running, a car driver would offer to take you and drop you off on his way; and because people are losing the sense of private property which is becoming collective.

On Sunday I had dinner with Mr d'Erlanger and his uncle,

---

[40] Lionel means himself here. While waiting to enlist, he was working as an accountant at the d'Erlanger bank.

an elderly baron. At the start of the meal, Mr d'Erlanger was called to the telephone and was told that an incendiary bomb had hit his uncle's house, 'but the fire brigade has arrived; I shall go and see and be back as soon as possible.' Forty-five minutes later, he was back; the fire had been under control from the very start. While he was out, the baron insisted that we continue to eat and, being the perfect host, was willing to speak about anything except his own house, which might well have been reduced to ashes. I hope I have taken in one of life's important lessons learned that evening.

Officially, because of the rules, no decision has been taken about my case. I'm still waiting; but unofficially, Mr d'Erlanger and Mr Palewski[41] believe it is only a question of time. They both hope that I might quite soon become an officer and then be very useful in liaison, though I feel that in this belief they may be overvaluing my ability.

Of course I'm not up-to-date with the latest developments in politics in either France or America, but some of the things I foresaw when I arrived in England seem to be coming about one by one. I was only trying to present parrain's ideas as faithfully and clearly as I could:

1. *The advantages of the French / British alliance,*
    a. *For France,*
    b. *For Britain,*

which must of course be made to work for the general good, together with any offers by the de Gaulle movement.

2. *The key role of the United States in the war.*
3. *The ways in which the Americans could offer further help.*
4. *The best use of current production capabilities.*

As happened last winter at Sciences Politiques, plagiarism

---

[41] Lionel met Mr Palewski at the home of Mr d'Erlanger, and he was always very kind to him.

seems to be serving me well. However, what follows is all my own.

It seems to me that the British government has not yet articulated clearly enough its war aims. The main attitude seems to be, 'First let's win the war, then we'll see.' This is a mistake. It seems to me that it can only be a good thing to have clear objectives in mind—in fact it's essential. Everyone acknowledges that Nazism in all its forms must be utterly destroyed, but this is only one element of a stable peace. On its own, it is not enough. We need something more constructive, and for the moment it is not clear what this is to be. I do so wish that the ideas explored by the Allied commission this winter would come true! And I believe it is more likely they will come about in the United States, so that efforts should be focused there.

I do so hope that after the war parrain will need a young secretary, and I would like to submit my application right now. You could add to the list of qualifications on my CV that I can now type thirty words per minute and take down eighty words per minute in shorthand. This anomaly should have been resolved by the time you receive this letter.

Many thanks for the cable you sent at the New Year. The last letter I received from you was dated 18 November.

Every day I appreciate Mr d'Erlanger a little bit more. He is so kind and looks after me so well—unlike your arriviste friend Dr X. If Dickens were alive, he would certainly make him a character in one of his stories. Puffed up with self-importance in both mind and body, thanks to the supposed significance of his official post, I have even known him to use the royal 'we'. No doubt he would find it quite natural to be addressed

as 'My Lord'. I fear his formerly considerable intelligence is
being blunted: he seems to have lost any sense of proportion
and objectivity. Everything relates back to him and to a small
circle of his friends who seem to be similarly self-satisfied.
Young P. is the only member of the family who still seems to
have some sense of proportion and to appreciate the funny side
of the situation and, being a philosophical eight-year-old, he is
rather enjoying it all.

I hope that by now Gérard feels more at home in the United
States and is doing better academically, and that Claude's
English has become fluent. Please give them both my fondest
regards.

With much love from
Lionel.

London, 2 February, 1941

Dear Mother,

It's the same old story: the last letter of yours that I received
was dated 6 December, and in it you said that the first part of
your tour was about to finish; you told me also about Gérard's
misbehaviour. Since then, nothing. Mr d'Erlanger assures me
the post is very bad: letters from his wife, when they come at
all, arrive erratically. I'm finding it hard to contain my growing
impatience for your next letter and I'm really looking forward
to hearing news of Paule and Renée.[42]

Mr Palewski showed me some reports from France where
the de Gaulle movement is growing fast. It's a great shame that
this organisation, which should, above all, be both symbolic

---

[42] These are my two daughters, who had stayed in France.

and idealistic, displays even in Britain all the shortcomings that one knows to be characteristic of French administrative systems—in some cases it seems these are even worse than usual. Nevertheless de Gaulle is quite a force in Britain, if only because he has considerable resources available to him that can make a difference right now to the conduct of the war, especially at sea. And moreover, de Gaulle's contribution is more than simply practical; his moral contribution will help to build peace in the future.

Now that people have had time to form clear judgments, opinion is divided in Britain on the subject of France between, on the one hand, the intellectual ruling minority and, on the other, the general population.

The general population are those who have rallied around Churchill and become the solid rock on which the wave of terror that submerged Europe has been shattered; they feel that the French government betrayed their people because they were too afraid to arm them and to create civil militias, and too afraid Paris would become a second Warsaw.

The ruling minority is much more aware of how much France has suffered in this war, and is displaying generosity of spirit in its understanding of what the armistice has meant to France.

So as far as the general public is concerned the armistice was an abomination, and only de Gaulle can save the honour of France. For the elite, de Gaulle is a very convenient tool because through him they have access to the part of the population which is not at the mercy of Nazi propaganda, and which offers hope of a fifth column matching Hitler's.

So opinions, although divided, are all in favour of 'Le

Général', which means that Britain feels able to act in consort with France—surely a key element of any future peace. In the last few days I have seen both Mr Robbins and Mr Cunliffe,[43] and also Major Cooper,[44] and they all agree that after the war France will of course regain its former position in Europe and the world.

And now to more specific matters, namely myself. I'm to be questioned by the department managing my enlistment, and they will let me know the outcome. If all goes well, and I really hope it will, it will only be a matter of days until I am at last enlisted in a British regiment. It has not been particularly pleasant to have to wait in London, but the time has not been wasted since I have now learned some basic accountancy and shorthand skills.

I will write again soon. Lots of love to you, and also to parrain and Claude.

Lionel.

---

[43] Both are important British economists.
[44] Chairman of the British Aluminium Company.

PART 2

Soldier and non-commissioned officer in the British Army

THE LETTERS THAT LIONEL MOSSÉRI WROTE during this period cover more or less exactly the years 1941 and 1942, from the time he joined the British army until the day he received his commission.

There were no particularly significant events during this span of time. He joined one of the best-known English regiments, the King's Royal Rifle Corps—also known as the 60th Rifles—in March 1941, and remained in the ranks for nine months; for most of this time, he was attached to the special platoon for those destined to train as officers.

He became a corporal at the start of December 1941, and three weeks later was sent to officer training for the first time. He was cruelly disappointed to be returned to his corps to spend more time as a non-commissioned officer, as it was felt he had not served long enough. Three months later he was chosen to attend the specialist training centre for officers in armoured units. He graduated with flying colours and was commissioned as second lieutenant on 17 December, 1942.

The first two years of army life were hard for Lionel. He learned his job from the bottom up, including peeling potatoes and sleeping on the ground for nearly a year. The training he underwent was extraordinarily intensive, moving from centre to centre and camp to camp. Having failed in its airborne attack against Britain, Germany turned its fire on the rest of Europe, including Russia, and on North Africa. The British government knew that with increasing support from the United States victory would eventually be their's; they were keen to avoid any unnecessary losses, and preferred to wait until they had all the cards in their hands before launching the final assault.

Montgomery had clearly understood that in modern warfare a man is no longer a pawn; just gun-fodder to be ordered blindly into battle. Soldiers are trained to be able to take decisions as necessary and to make superhuman efforts at key moments. Training a true soldier of this kind is a lengthy, methodical and specialised undertaking.

Lionel hated marching. It was his misfortune to end up in the British regiment with the quickest marching pace. Two years later, he was winning sprinting races in his battalion. He became expert at gymnastics and jiu-jitsu, and as a mechanic able to service motorcycles, cars and tanks. His correspondence does not refer to it, but during this time he also trained as a commando. A friend of ours, Mr Albert Grand, saw him several times in London and recounted a number of good stories from this period.

On one occasion, the head of their unit assembled his men somewhere near London and said to them, 'Gentlemen, please hand over all your identity papers and your money. Today is Monday. I will meet you at noon this coming Friday in front of Aberdeen station in Scotland. Please be on time. You may do whatever you like: borrow or steal a bicycle, a car or a locomotive; find food and lodging as you wish. Only one thing is forbidden: you may not say that you are commandos. Goodbye, gentlemen. Please do not be late for our rendezvous.'

Another time, the head of the unit told them, 'You must learn how to make a surprise attack on a divisional HQ, taking its personnel and all documents. Right now there is an excellent opportunity. An American division has just disembarked a few miles from here. Their HQ is guarded in the normal way, but you'll find a way around that. Please bring me the personnel and papers by tomorrow noon; bring the men here unharmed.'

This was done: within a few hours, the team had surreptitiously gained access to the office of the general himself and shouted, 'Hands up!' The American officers, fearful and amazed, were escorted to the commandos' HQ, where the operation was explained to them. They then started laughing and exclaiming, 'Nice one, dude!'

In fact, commando training exercises were not always as harmless as this. There were sometimes operations or surprise attacks on the French coast, or indeed inland. Two friends of ours[45] were told confidentially a few years later that Lionel took part in three landings in France, during one of which he was nearly taken prisoner by a German patrol passing only fifty metres away from him.

But these things were not really significant. For Lionel, the greatest trial at this time was that his career did not advance faster. He envied friends who had the good fortune to be at Dunkirk and rose to the rank of officer after only a few months in the lower ranks. The losses had become less severe, so the army needed far fewer young officers. In order to speed things along, he tried to transfer to the Indian Army, but he was kept back because he was thought to be of more use to the home

[45] Mr Albert Grand and Miss Terré.

army. He was heartbroken at being asked to repeat his non-commissioned officer training, fearing that he would miss out on the 'excitement' that generally happened in the spring.[46]

It would be wrong, however, to think he regretted having to spend so much time in the lower ranks. 'These men are truly magnificent, both in mind and body'.[47] He was pleased to have had the opportunity to meet them and to get to know them well. He felt sorry for the young officers—and there were not many of these—who came straight from higher education and had not had the opportunities he enjoyed to mix with such a wide range of society. As a result of this long and close relationship with the troops, he became devoted to his men, who, in turn were fervently loyal to him.

Occasionally, he engages with wider issues in his correspondence. He explains how the British had managed, in two years' training for the final assault, to solve the problem that had defeated France in 1939: maintaining the morale of inactive troops.

He also tackled a key British issue: secondary school reform. Many have suggested that the old public school system—which trained all those who built up the Empire and who ended up dominating the fields of politics, the press, industry, commerce and finance—should be discontinued, because too bound up with the aristocracy. On the other hand, it could be argued that it should be developed and opened up to the less wealthy.

He refers frequently to the issues that will be important in the years ahead: the need to start defining a future peace; researching how to set up an economic system to provide opportunities for the generosity many people wish to show as

[46] Letter, 6 January 1942.
[47] Letter, 26 August 1941.

opposed to founding one on individualist, selfish desires. In Britain at war, he could sense an altruism which could shape a new era.[48]

A few female figures feature fleetingly in his diary. He was drawn to the conversation of girls and young women, but he avoided their company: a pleasant evening spent dancing left him feeling despondent for days afterwards. Only one woman truly stands out—a childhood friend, barely older than he, whom he called V. She had recently married, and her husband had 'done wonderfully well, partly due to considerable losses in France; he had been promoted extremely quickly.'[49]

V. was intelligent and cultured; witty and serious. Lionel bore her a deep and pure affection. He sometimes forgot that he might compromise her reputation, had it not been so unassailable. He found out that she was living with her parents-in-law in a small town and decided to visit her when on leave. He was delighted to spend time with a friend who reminded him of good times past. He arrived at dusk, not quite sure of V.'s address. He himself was unconcerned that he might arouse comment, but created a sensation in the village, going from door to door asking if anyone knew the address of Mrs P., the young French wife of a British officer. A few months later, on hearing at the last minute that he would be able to spend Christmas in London, he sent a casual but affectionate telegram, 'I am spending Christmas in town, please come and celebrate with me.'

All the letters from this period are lively and alert; full of wit, evocative descriptions, and amusing stories about his colleagues and his superiors. I have in a few places cut out repetitions, or passages which are only of interest to the family.

---

[48] Letter, 16 March, 1941.
[49] Letter, 19 October, 1941.

London, 8 February, 1941

Dear Mother,

I was interviewed the day before yesterday. This morning I had my medical. The day after tomorrow I go to join my regiment: the 'King's Royal Rifle Corps'. Mr d'Erlanger tells me it is one of the best in the British army. I am to spend three or four months in the ranks and then, if I am up to it, I shall be sent to a platoon of trainee officers. I should then receive my first stripe, after a period of intensive training—the length of which is not set.

I am delighted, especially as Mr Palewski has assured me that there will be interesting work available to me once I am an officer.

Recruitment is extremely well organised, especially the medical. Each conscript is examined in turn by six Harley Street specialists, who would no doubt charge £5 each if they were seen privately. So I have already cost the British government £30 this morning. However, in return they are getting an A1 specimen.

After the medical, I was sworn in. It was an impressive ceremony, I thought, but then I am sentimental. The commanding officer was rather blasé and seemed to find the whole thing quite routine. The poor man is obviously extremely busy.

The final element in the rite was receiving my first pay packet. For the first months I shall be paid 2/6 per day. If I were married, or if I could prove I was living with someone, I would have received an additional 17/- per week, but unfortunately I don't qualify.

I went to see Mr Newell who gave me fantastic letters of recommendation and some good advice. He also renewed his standing invitation to me, and suggested I take him up on it next time I am on leave. There is only one cloud in this otherwise blue sky. At Newquay I saw a regiment training: in addition to the 60km marches, the men run races of five to eight kilometres twice a week. That will be at least as testing as it was at Gresham's, for I doubt the sergeants are any gentler than the school prefects.

There are several rugby fields and golf courses at Newquay, and on Saturday and Sunday afternoons most of the men and officers go there in great crowds. As a result, the pubs are relatively empty. As you can see, the men are both physically and morally in great shape. Of course, the British army does not have the traditions of the French army, but on the other hand it is spared the ancient customs that are the inevitable corollary. Everything is new, modern and full of energy.

I have packed up my things, using a suitably large number of mothballs, and Mr d'Erlanger will keep them for me. He really is wonderfully kind, and I hope I can be of service to him one of these days.

I am nervous and excited at this new stage of my life, and I hope with all my heart that I shall do well. At any rate, I shall do my very best. I shall not give up for an instant—I want to be a good soldier and a good officer.

Tonight, before going to sleep, I shall re-read all the letters you have written to me since Father's death, and although we are six thousand kilometres apart, it is with you that I shall spend my last evening before going to join my future comrades. These three months in London have not been much fun, it can now be admitted, and I can't tell you how many times my ears have anxiously strained to hear an approving or reproving 'Lionel!'

I will write again soon.

Lionel.

23 February, 1941

Dearest Mother,

I've now been a squaddie for two weeks. I do hope you will forgive me for not having written since I left London, as these two weeks have not exactly been a holiday.

We are garrisoned... kilometres away from London which is very pleasant. Our accommodation is a very nice sports club which has been requisitioned, so we have splendid facilities for playing rugby and tennis, and for boxing.

My comrades are all under twenty years old and we are quite a mixed lot. The rule in the British army is that no one can become an officer before spending at least three months in the ranks, which can lead to some quite comic and even ridiculous situations. We are sleeping in what used to be the banqueting room, and the first night our company included the son of a general, a student at Cambridge, and former pupils from Harrow, Winchester and Charterhouse, while the rest were from what the English call—and I don't know if this is a subtle irony, or simply a lack of awareness of the paradox the term sometimes implies—'the working class'.

I will start at the beginning. At 2 o'clock in the afternoon, I was lost in... with my sleeping bag and a small suitcase, asking a taxi driver to tell me the way. This lovely fellow had been in my regiment in the last war, and he offered to drive me there for nothing, as he had nothing better to do. He only accepted a glass of beer in payment.

Inside the barracks, the first thing I was given was my pay book, and then my kit. Two weeks on I'm still agreeably surprised by the quality, the comfort and the simplicity of it all. Socks, shirts, underclothes, shoes, sports kit, everything was immaculate; and half an hour later I and all the other new arrivals were sent off to the sports club.

The first three days were the worst. The rules say that you have to do nothing but chores, and I should have done twice as much as I did. I think I now know every single kind of potato there is. For entertainment, we spent the evening naming our kit and learning how to fold and pack it all.

The next three days were spent learning to march, and it really isn't easy. Unfortunately, my regiment is the one with the fastest pace in the British army: 180 steps per minute for ceremonies, 160 steps on parade, 120 to 130 when marching. Throughout, the arms also move regularly, and must be swung from the shoulder. Man was not made to walk that fast.

We have just finished the second week which was very interesting. The sergeant has a remarkably wide vocabulary; even the most hardened recruits blush under the full force of it. However, in the evenings, once we have done an hour's boxing in our so-called free time, we are allowed to go out. The boxing instructor, formerly a champion in the Indian Army, has already given me a few bruises to remember him by, and I don't think he has any in return. Tomorrow we will start physical fitness and weapon handling. The sergeant looks very pleased at the prospect, so I really wonder what is going to hit us. However, as you may have gathered if you've been reading between the lines, I'm having a wonderful time. I don't need to think; the physical exertions are exhausting, but studying Roman law was more exhausting. I have delightful comrades and the general air of optimism probably comes from the feeling that at last we are able to do something to counteract the ghastly nightmare we have all been living with for the last few years.

I am now in a room with three other fellows, and one of them, who was at Charterhouse, I like particularly. He is very young—officially eighteen. We are very lucky to be in the same room, since it seems that most of the irritations of life as a soldier are incidental and derive from those who poison the existence of others, and would do so even in a luxury hotel, through laziness, untidiness or theft. The other two in my room are also very nice: one is a theology student, and the other, who was also at public school, was working in his father's large industrial company. The inspecting officer was very amused when he visited our room. 'It's a club, complete with New Statesman and Times!' But he advised that we should avoid living in splendid isolation. The fact is that we need to watch our step fairly carefully to avoid antagonising some of our other comrades. Parrain will remember, I expect, the conversation we once had on the way to Saint Cloud. I was saying that the British public school system, although excellent for those who can afford it, could exacerbate social differences. It seems I was right: there is a growing body of opinion in England opposed to the system. Sadly, it is the schools themselves that are criticised rather than the fact that only 5%

of children are able to study there. I am quite convinced—and so is Mr Newell—that public school provides by far the better education. French lycées are not in the same league, and the American imitation does not measure up either. It would be a huge shame if England were to lose all these schools, which produced the men who built the Empire and those who will rebuild the world tomorrow. I really hope that instead they will manage to find a way to admit a larger number of children.

Talking of studies, I do hope that Gérard is now reconciled to the idea of studying and that he and Claude are both well. I often think of them and I miss them.

Please give them a hug from me, and also one to parrain. The last letter I received was the one with 'admonishments', and now I would even welcome another one of those.

I will write again soon, and lots of love,

Lionel.

Harrow, 16 March, 1941

Dearest Mother,

Your letter of 24 February has reached me in record time— the one you asked me not to throw away even if I found it boring. How could you possibly think that I would not avidly read each word you sent me from such a long way away, how could you think that I don't find every line you write to be a treasure chest to be feverishly explored? First, you say you are worried I should be suffering for no reason; the answer is that the only suffering that counts, during this war and the years for which we are separated, is the fact that I'm not with you and unfortunately it is you who is worrying about me. You see, I'm so selfish that I'm asking you to relieve me of this worry, so please promise that you will not have any more such concerns about me.

I am living here among those who are happiest in Europe since they live neither in the neurotic fever or atmosphere of Italian fascism nor under Nazism. And of these, I am one of the most fortunate, since I know whatever happens, you are safe, and you will not be hungry, no bomb will fall and hurt you or destroy in a few seconds the life you have built up or your savings. I am among friends and not among strangers, as are most of the free French. I'm in a country I love and for which I have a deep admiration. My admiration is greater than ever right now, because this fierce battle has given it a new spirit, which will give birth to a new era. It is perhaps paradoxical, but this bloody conflict is giving birth to a dream of peace, of hard work, of love and brotherhood. I have been reading books on political economy, and whether they are liberal or socialist, I find they all more or less agree that 'material profit is the best motor for human activity'. When I read this last winter, I was doubtful; the artist, the musician and the priest are not motivated by the desire for gold. Now I have evidence before my very eyes that there are things far more powerful than money which is spent in vast amounts every day and seems to have lost its value; a value which was only ever subjective and contrived in any case.

I know you are not very keen on my digressions, but this is what I'm thinking and what is inspiring my dreams of a fine and wonderful future, so I hope that for once you might forgive me, especially if I include them amongst practical information.

To start with, some good news: I and fifteen others have been assigned to a so-called 'potential officers' unit'. This is not in any way official, but unofficially it means the colonel has selected us to be sent to officer training at some stage. On a practical level, this means 75% of the unpleasant aspects of being a squaddie are no longer a problem, since we now have our own separate lodgings in a pretty little house, and especially because all those included in this little group are generally well brought up and well educated. On the other hand, the colonel expects faultless discipline and a high state of fitness. He waxed lyrical, 'your bodies are now your most precious asset, so please work on them constantly.' In order to help us, he has allocated us a sergeant and a corporal from the Guards. You will appreciate the full significance of this when I tell you a story about two men who were at the end of a five-year tour with the foreign legion and joined the Guards. Two weeks later, they committed suicide because the training was too harsh. Every day, we do one hour of boxing and one hour of gym; on Saturdays we also play rugby, and on Wednesdays we march ten to fifteen miles carrying a 75lb pack. And of course we also have as many parades and military exercises as our torturer-in-chief chooses to inflict on us.

This life is pleasant. In fact, it would be perfect if I had a few hours truly to myself from time to time in which I could read, write and think in peace. But one can't have everything. I must confess my intellectual life is in a poor state; I've done no serious reading, as it's really not possible and, what is worse, I can't even summon up the desire to climb out of the rut I have fallen into. My comrades are all delightful but they are suffering in the same way.

Longstaffe (my friend from Charterhouse) invited me last Sunday to go and spend the day at his parents' home in London. They were charming. After a lunch as good as the best I had in Paris, they took me to the theatre, and afterwards to supper at Claridge's. It was the most wonderful day, not only because of the lovely things we did, but above all because they were so kind and thoughtful. His mother said to me, 'Do come as often as you would like, and since your parents are in America, maybe we can take their place a little bit.' His father took me aside and said, 'And if ever you are in need of money…' What was so marvellous was that it was all most sincere and unostentatious.

This afternoon, Longstaffe and I went for a walk. In front of the others, as we are potential officers, we behave with great dignity, but the two of us alone were behaving like a couple of children when a car stopped near us and a lady of about fifty climbed out and said, 'If you've not yet had tea, would you do me the honour of coming in and having a cup of tea at my house?' We accepted enthusiastically and were taken to a delightful little Tudor-style house. We sat in the sitting-room in front of a roaring fire, admiring the Louis XVI furniture and the paintings by Corot, and drinking tea at least as good as the China tea you had in Paris. We spent a very happy hour and then our hostess insisted on driving us back to the barracks.

I have told you about this because it is typical of the kind of thing that frequently happens.

I am trying to spend as little as possible, but life is very expensive. Before enlisting, I spent £7 on kit, and since then, I have asked Mr Newell to send me £5 per month. He and Mr d'Erlanger agree this is not excessive. In francs, it seems a lot, but in fact it is just the cost of the extra meal I have every day with a few friends. My wages as a soldier cover all my other expenses.

Please send me news of Claude and Gérard; I had news of parrain from Mr Harriman,[50] to whom I spoke on the phone.

Any day now, Mr Palewski will be leaving for the United States. I hope you will have a chance to meet him, as he is a wonderful person.

I often think of you and I send you lots and lots of love.
Lionel.

Harrow, 3 April, 1941

Dearest Mother,

My turn now to shout for joy: letters, at last! I have received three in the last ten days. All mine go by airmail, so I don't understand why so many of them don't reach you. Now that I am in the army, maybe the censor keeps a less careful eye on me and is letting my post through more easily.

I'm so pleased to know your tour is proving both useful and enjoyable; you and parrain seem to be particularly good at combining the two.

Life continues here. It's a bit less interesting now that we are on the treadmill and have used up all that Harrow has to offer. I think I shall be in the ranks for about another six weeks before going off for officer training at about the beginning of June, and then it will be four to six months until I am an officer.

I don't suppose I should be ashamed of this really, but often when I am writing to you I stop and wonder what on earth I

[50] United States ambassador to Russia.

could tell you about. Even though we are so far apart, I both feel and know there are ways we communicate that are more lasting and more effective than pen and paper. I feel, for the things that really matter, neither you nor I have any need to write them down. So all I can describe are the little details of everyday life: chatting with my friends, the ongoing silent tussles with certain sergeants, the things I do in my free time, and, for what they are worth, my thoughts for the future.

The colonel is dedicated to producing the highest possible level of physical fitness in his potential officers, and this is bearing fruit—unfortunately this is not true in terms of discipline. In the novel *Suzanne et le Pacifique*, the author describes one of the results of living in an entirely natural state: 'Small round hard things began to grow on my arms.' This description would not do justice to me and most of my friends: we are hardened all over, so that the mattress on the floor seems to me to be as soft as a Sultan's sofa, and I am not even intimidated by Rydyard in my room. Rydyard boxed for Winchester and boxing is his one and only passion. So whenever he feels like it, he practises— generally on the poor chap who is unfortunate enough to be standing next to him. To start with, I was as useless as a poor punch bag, furious but impotent, whereas now, if Rydyard has a go at me, he leaves no marks. I have two other roommates, one of whom is a happy-go-lucky sportsman; he has too much money, not many brains, a splendid body, and a brilliant sense of balance and composure—so he is a first-class athlete. He is a charming fellow and everyone likes him, but in some ways he is quite shallow. The fourth is Longstaffe, of whom I have already written so you know a little about him. He is tall and elegant, supple, intelligent, shrewd and very cultured. We had started to become good friends, but very sadly he has suddenly decided for family reasons to change regiments, so in a few days time he is going to leave. This is a real shame; not only was he delightful company, he was also the only person with whom I could have really serious and fruitful discussions – my current substitute for reading, as I no longer have either the inclination or, particularly, the time to read much.[51]

In theory, we have plenty of free time: from five until ten each evening, except the days when we are on duty. But every day we have to do an hour's boxing and also spend at least an hour cleaning our kit; twice a week we practise target-shooting, and we have a certain amount of theory to work on. As a result, five hours dwindle to two, and in that time it is quite difficult to read because there is nowhere to do so comfortably, and as you know I'm not keen on noise.

Our house is delightful but it has practically no furniture, so that I have to read Keynes and Pirou sitting on the floor, using a suitcase as a table; this makes it difficult to create the atmosphere of peace and concentration that I sadly still need, but I hope soon to learn to do without.

I go to London nearly every Sunday afternoon, and Mr d'Erlanger continues to be extremely friendly and hospitable.

Thank you so much for your understanding about how much I'm spending. I have already told you that I withdraw about £5 per month, most of which I spend on food. The kit is very good and my only expenditure is on socks, as I seem to get through them frighteningly quickly; my shoes are first-class and my feet are in perfect condition. I still have £140 deposited with Mr Newell, so I shall be all right for a little while. Please don't worry about me, either on this account or

---

[51] Longstaffe in fact moved not to a different regiment but to a different battalion. He was wounded in Italy, won the Military Cross and went to join his battalion in Greece, where he died, aged twenty-two.

on any other. I am feeling really well. 'My' bomb landed more than 500 metres away from me when I was in London. The krauts have not yet come to visit where I am staying.

Please thank parrain very much for his letter. I'm so pleased you have good news from France. I hope the winter of 1942 will be the last one that Renée and Paule will have to spend with les boches as uninvited guests, and that we shall have thrown them out by the end of 1943.

People are in very good spirits here. Everyone is contributing to the national effort. You would be astonished to see the women (very many of them) splendidly uniformed and equipped, doing meticulous work in all three services, as well as the less romantic but extremely useful work that they do in accountancy, catering, and so on—so that the men can be freed up for active service. It will take a while for the results of this to become clear, but the day will come–as sure as the sun rises—when it will be our turn to land on the beaches; I pity those who will face one of our bayonet charges.

I'm looking forward to the reward for the many arduous hours we have spent training with this weapon. Please continue to send armaments—just get them here and we will do the rest.

I will write again soon, dearest Mother.

Lots of love from your

Lionel.

15 May, 1941

Dearest Mother,

Since the beginning of this month, my company has been camping and training hard. Life in the open air is very healthy, but it takes a few days to get used to it. We are camping in a very pretty part of England, but we could just as well be in France or America had we been brought here in a plane by night. The nearest village has 120 inhabitants and is more than three kilometres from our camp, and the nearest town is twelve kilometres away—it has a cinema and, strangely enough, an excellent hotel. There is no transport, either bus or train, and we are not allowed to stray further than two miles from the camp. So you see we are leading a monastic life. Reveille is sounded at a quarter past six in the morning and the water is very cold, which is just as well, since otherwise I would not be awake until lunchtime. We go on parade at half past eight, and every day, after inspection, one or two fellows whose beard resisted the razor and cold water are summoned to the police tent. I have bought a mechanical dry shaver called Viceroy, a bit like my electric razor except that the power is created by pressing a lever. It works very well so, what with that and my sleeping bag, I am living in luxury, much more so than some officers. The food is quite good, but it could be improved if the cooks mastered their job better; at any rate there is enough of it. We are still doing a great deal of marching, and practising quite a few manoeuvres. As a result, we are becoming true soldiers. This is the kind of military life of which I had a vague idea when I was reading the first scene of *Iphigénie*, which describes two men walking around the camp between the tents during the quiet of the night. Being on guard duty at Harrow was very boring, but here it actually makes a difference. As well as the thrill of knowing one is as clean and gleaming as possible when one goes on guard duty, the double ration of cartridges we are given shows that we have some responsibility. Last week I had a real fright. It was three in the morning and I was patrolling around the camp; suddenly I heard the sound of steps quite close by, so I called out as we are supposed to. No answer. I called out again, and the noise started up again. I was about to shoot when suddenly I saw a quite distinct shape... it was a cow! The rest of my turn of duty was peaceful. The stars in the sky were gorgeous, and slowly, each little light went out until there was only one left, the most beautiful; it too was about to go out when I was relieved. In my report, I wrote, 'All is well'.

I haven't yet had my official interview. I'm on the list, awaiting my turn with reasonable patience. I'm enjoying this simple life free of responsibility, of worries, of exams, although I'm pleased to know that things will get better. I have received the £300 from Egypt. You need not have sent this to me. I had enough money; my account with Mr Newell should last at least another eighteen months. Mr Newell and Mr d'Erlanger have both adopted me. Parrain is very lucky to have friends who like him so much that they will look after his stepson.

Now that summertime has come, I will be able to write to you more often, because in the evening when we get back it will be light for longer.

Dearest Mother, who knows how soon we shall see each other?

Lionel.

2 June, 1941

Dearest Mother,

Our special platoon has now returned to camp after two weeks on manoeuvres.

When I got back, I was told that I would be meeting the selection board next time it convened. If I pass—and I have every reason to hope that I will—I shall be sent to an officer training centre, probably at the beginning of July; I should graduate from there in October with my first stripe. In fact, everything is happening rather as it would have done had I stayed in France, where I would have been called up at twenty and, with some preparatory military training, would have been sent straight to the platoon for reserve officer cadets.

However, there is one important difference. Having spent four months in the ranks, I have learned not only about military matters, but about sociological issues in particular— knowledge I would not otherwise have had and which I sorely needed. Pascal wrote, 'Most people live either in the past or in the future so that one can say that they never actually live.' Thanks to the last few months, I now realise that I have had the most wonderful opportunities in my life, which will open many doors for me.

I have also discovered quite how sheltered and happy our life was in our little world. Too sheltered perhaps, as I feel that my outlook was very limited—in England to public schools and to Oxford, and in France to Sciences Politiques.

Even some friends from the law faculty seem to be the exception rather than the rule: I didn't really understand them and their life seemed to me to be somewhat unusual, whereas in fact I now realise I was the unusual animal. When I came back to camp, I found your letter of 15 May (the seventh since 6 March). I read and re-read it a number of times and I showed some of it to Mr d'Erlanger, whom I saw yesterday.

I know that when the armistice was signed you were very hopeful of Pétain, so I fully understand how disappointed you must be about his new political plans. It's fortunate that he says he is responsible only to History!

I don't pretend to understand all the things that lie behind his politics, but I think there really should be a code of honour regulating the way these things are managed.

In spite of recent events, I remain firmly optimistic since nothing can break the joint strength of English spirit and American equipment. The way in which the Navy has avenged HMS *Hood* is typical of the mood here. 'You can strike us hard; not only will we take it, but we will strike you even harder in return.'

I shall go on leave immediately after my selection board. I will spend three days with Mr Newell and three days with Mr d'Erlanger.

I now don't know which I'm longing for most: a letter from you, my leave, or my selection board. I think if the post were working better, I would not be terribly keen to leave the camp, but sometimes I do feel quite lonely and, as Beatrice said, 'I need a bit of kindness'! By this you may understand 'I need my mother', and if I can't have her then a bit of understanding and friendship.

It's quite hard to keep up a mask of coolness and virility and when in fact . . . quite a number of my friends are engaged, and yet it's the letters from their mothers that they await with the greatest impatience; you can imagine how eagerly I wait to hear from mine, since I'm not even engaged!

I'll write again soon, dearest Mother.

Your Lionel.

26 August, 1941

Dearest Mother,

At last, for the first time since I enlisted, I'm going to be able to write to you often, at great length, and regularly, which I haven't been able to do, especially recently.

For the first time for four months, I'm no longer sleeping in a tent with seven other people; for the first time for four months, I shan't simply feel like going to sleep after going on parade. The intensive training period is finished: we are now fully prepared soldiers and we have been dispatched to guard an airfield.

As far as comfort is concerned, we are certainly no better off. Once again we are in the middle of nowhere, twelve kilometres from the nearest town. The airfield itself is still being built. For the moment there are no planes. The building is going well, however, and we have our work cut out. In addition to guard duties, we are building defences all round the area: barbed wire, trenches and concrete shelters. It all sounds rather grand, but in fact it means I am doing ground works. However, it's all very good experience as we are learning both the theory of where the best defensive positions are, and also, just as importantly, the practical difficulties of actually building them.

Although we are working hard, it is less tiring than the training we have been doing recently. Because of censorship, I was not able to describe our activities in detail, but I suppose you may be able to read in the newspapers in America about some of the ways in which the British Army is trained. Now that time is all just a memory life is easier—one doesn't simply forget having to run seven kilometres every day. I have at least three evenings a week completely free. So I have been able to rent a room in a farm nearby, which is the only building anywhere near the camp, and I shall be able to start reading again and to write to you as I have been wishing to do. I had a letter from parrain yesterday, and ten days ago I received a long epistle from the whole family. I shall reply to Claude and Gérard separately, since this letter will not reach you very far ahead of the ones I plan to write to them tomorrow. For the moment please just give them all my love and tell them I think of them all the time.

I have so many things to say to you that I have wanted to write for the last three weeks that I hardly know where to start.

Maybe I shouldn't reproach myself with that. I was so touched by what you wrote in your last letter, 'For myself, I simply love you and I find time goes very slowly without you.' I would echo your words as they say exactly what I feel.

Our company has been firmly assigned to this airfield, so I shall only leave it when I go to officer training, and there too shall be able to write you regularly. I don't know when this will happen. Two months ago I was judged to be a suitable candidate for the training at the OCTU,[52] so I am waiting for my turn, which the captain said should come soon even though there is a less urgent need for new officers than there was last

[52] Officer Cadet Training Unit.

year. However, I have no regrets about spending so much time in the ranks. Some days have been hard and unpleasant, some very difficult, but I would have been very sorry to have missed them.

Now I have some hope of becoming a real leader of men and not simply a puppet exercising an authority conferred only by virtue of a hierarchy backing him up. I will try, even if I never get it completely right, to be the kind of leader my men want and deserve. For these men are truly magnificent, both in mind and body. They never complain, they accept everything: waiting, mud, chores, guard duty and bombings; yet they are so sensitive, so human. I want to be worthy of them just as my officers are, in particular my captain. I will just tell you the story of something that happened recently.

Six comrades and I were throwing loaded grenades during training. The captain was present. One of the thrown grenades failed to explode. Five seconds went by, then ten, then fifteen. 'Stay here in safety,' the captain ordered. 'I'll go and see.' As calm as if he were simply on an exercise—even though every step he took could have made the grenade explode—he climbed out of the trench, walked towards the grenade, examined it carefully and defused it. He then came back to the trench just as calmly and turned to one of my comrades, 'It's your turn, I think.' This man had faced death as surely as any flying ace in the RAF, without seeking glory, just doing his duty. I don't like to dwell too long on the story—it makes me emotional.

I'm being called, so I have to stop. Lots of love,
Your Lionel.

1 September, 1941

Dearest Mother,

It was my birthday yesterday, and I had an extremely pleasant time. To start with, it was Sunday and the weather was wonderful, which it has not often been recently. I'm sure it was your good wishes and your thoughts that helped to make the day so lovely for me—again, thank you so much.

Until now, or at least since I left Harrow five months ago, I haven't written much about military life itself; I thought perhaps it was time I did so. I'm sure you will understand that if my life seems quite harsh, it is only so in order to provide good training, and in fact I could not be happier.

You will remember that in France one of the main concerns of the government and the high command was to combat general boredom among the troops. They therefore stationed any regiments who were not actually on the front line in towns well behind the lines; but the soldiers got terribly bored, as they didn't organise anything for themselves, and just waited for others to supply them with day centres such as the one you helped with at Creil.

The British government has not made the same mistake. They have a deliberate policy of sending the majority of the troops to spend five or six months on camp, away from any town. Most of their time is spent on manoeuvres and exercises, some time is spent on sports, and then what the squaddies call 'spit and polish'. The British soldier should always look impeccably turned out; as I have often written, the kit is superb, but to keep it in good shape, you have to spend at least one hour a day on its maintenance. Woe betide anyone whose socks have holes, or whose trousers are missing buttons at weekly inspection. When I am on guard duty—and this now happens quite often—I have to spend at least two hours getting ready. So you see, we don't have a great deal of free time: just enough to have about two or three evenings a week completely free, but certainly not enough to get bored.

You were very disappointed I haven't sent you a photo. I haven't set foot in a town for at least six weeks. You could mention to Gérard, who seems to want to spread his wings, that since my return from leave more than two months ago, I literally haven't said a single word to a girl. It's not that there aren't any around, even here; you can always find one if you really look. I don't wish to be a snob, but I do find it so unrewarding to spend time with a girl who doesn't have at least some education and culture; and even if I could find one such, I really don't wish to fall in love; I don't think any soldier should allow himself that luxury or even weakness. Here is a story I haven't yet told you:

A couple of weeks before I went on leave, I went out early one Sunday morning with a book, some sardines and some bread, hoping to find somewhere to lie in the sun for the whole day. I had walked scarcely two kilometres along the road when I came across a car that had broken down. The driver was attempting to change the wheel but was having no luck; between the two of us, we did manage it, and the young lady (you probably guessed it) asked where I was going and what I was planning to do. She thought that there might be better ways to spend a Sunday and invited me to come with her to Wimbledon to spend the day with friends, promising to drive me back in the evening, as she had to go my way anyway. She was right, it was all perfect: delicious dinner, a wonderful game of tennis, a tea dance and an excellent supper—I was back at camp just before 10 o'clock. But for the following two days, I was despondent. I had been momentarily thrown off balance, and I have promised myself I won't let it happen again.

Please, if you would, send me V.'s address,[53] as I would very much like to see her again.

At the end of the month we are moving into our winter quarters in a town where life will certainly be less bucolic and austere than it is here, where it's becoming quite monotonous. There is one redeeming feature: life in the army is particularly good for those who are unmarried and have no dependents. At a purely physical level, the issue of survival and any such worries are more or less dealt with, so one can make the most of opportunities for intellectual work. I spend every free evening at the farm, comfortably isolated from the rest of the world, in a little room that is both pleasant and warm, where I can read, dream and study even more enjoyably than I did in Paris, where I first learned to study, and there was the constant pressing need to cover the syllabus and face exams.

Please thank parrain very much for his letter. I'm so proud of the wonderful work he's doing, and delighted to learn that his efforts are meeting with such success; I'm touched to hear that he is thinking of me so much and still trying to help me, even from so far away. I shall see Lady Abingdon as soon as she arrives. Mr d'Erlanger will be able to get her address for me.

With all my love,

Lionel.

---

[53] 'V.' was a great friend from his childhood. She had recently married an English officer, who was killed two years later in Burma.

Sunday, 19 October, 1941

Dearest Mother,

I have just enjoyed a perfect leave: as perfect a leave as can be when I am so far from you. I spent two days with Mr Newell, and two days with V.—at last I managed to get her address from Mr Cooper.

Of course she isn't V. any more, but Mrs Porter. Her husband Philip is a captain in a well-known regiment, in which he has done wonderfully well, partly due to considerable losses in France, and he has been promoted extremely quickly.

V. left France in March with some difficulty, and found in Lisbon that she had lots of new little nephews. I spent many hours listening to a story both fascinating and very sad, about lots of people we used to know, and about France under the occupation.

Now I'm back at camp, all too soon it seems. The time went so fast. Here, we train hard during the day, but it is interesting, and every evening is free. By extraordinary good luck, there has been a political economy lecture series during my stay, so I've been going to those. I was also advised, indeed practically ordered, by one of my superior officers to learn to dance!

I have mixed feelings about the tour you are now planning. Don't you think you need a bit of a rest? Of course the last one was so successful that I can see why you want to do another, and I really hope it will go very well. On behalf of all those who will benefit from your efforts (is this presumptuous of me?), may I thank you in advance.

I spoke with Lady Abingdon about the telegram you

received from General de Gaulle, and she said that when she
had spoken to him he was well aware of all the good work that
parrain is doing. As I told you before, I was hoping to be able to
join the Indian Army. Unfortunately the War Office decided
a little while ago to keep their 'potential officers' and to send
them off to training, sending the very best first, rather than
observing seniority as before.

When I went for my second selection board, with fifty
others, unfortunately the general took a great liking to me and
insisted that I should stay in the British army itself, and he put
me at the top of the list—he said that I would be more useful
here than elsewhere. So as a result I'm still in competition with
many others, even though my name is at the top of the list, and
I may well have to wait another three months. I don't know
why everything is conspiring to build my character.

Mr d'Erlanger is still extremely kind to me. He treats me
more like a favourite nephew than a young man he didn't know
a year ago.

I will write again soon and I send you lots and lots of love.
Your Lionel.

44 Upper Grosvenor Street, S. W. 1.
6 January, 1942.

Dearest Mother,

I am on leave again, for the last time now until June.

On Tuesday evening I was still a corporal, and then on
Wednesday, just like that, I found myself changed into an
officer cadet. I start officer cadet school on 9 January for a

course that will last about seven months. In my last letter I told you how cross I was with the old general who wanted to keep me in the British army and stop me going off to India, but I think he must have given me a very high score for me to be promoted so quickly because… oh, bother! I'm not allowed to give you any figures!

After the first flush of excitement when I got the news, I suddenly found that I wasn't nearly as happy about it as I had thought I would be. It made me realise how much I miss you, and that I will only be happy again when we are together once more. Everything I have learned in England has all gone by the board, and I'm writing with no self-control, as I must have done when I was twelve in my first week at school—except that then I had more pride than I have now.

However, I was very displeased with your letter of 21 December which has just arrived. You really must not worry about me. By all accounts life in the British army is a lot easier than in the French. Not physically of course, because the training is such hard work, but the atmosphere is different. And now you know that whatever happens, I shall not see active service for the next seven months. I myself would have preferred to, because there is usually some excitement in the spring and now I fear I shall miss out on it, but no doubt you will feel much happier.

I have been far from you for a year now, and living in a very different way. Every day, I appreciate more and more the care you took as I was growing up. Don't worry, I think you were just strict enough with me, setting limits and so on, but you did no more than was necessary. I would like you to know how grateful I am to you.

I have been rereading your letter and I'm more and more thankful to the old general. I had not realised that you were so concerned by my hopes of joining the Indian Army; from now on, I promise I will ask you first.

All my very fondest love,

Lionel.

14 January, 1942

Dearest Mother,

I have been at OCTU for nearly a week now. It's in a lovely spot and I can't imagine it could be any more pleasant. There is quite an interesting little town nearby and we are once again housed in great comfort—not that we have to pay for it, as it is mostly provided by the army. The food is better than we have been used to—well prepared and well presented. I have a comfortable and cheerful room and, wonder of wonders; I have a bed with a mattress for the first time in nine months (except for one three-week period). For five months, I shall live like a prince, unless, of course, I am demoted to the ranks.

Our colonel is a charming man, intelligent and cultured, and he has a wealth of experience. The other officers seem to be first-class too, as do our instructors.

In some ways, I have gone back to my early days as a young recruit. I don't think I've ever been through such tough training. We all thought we were experienced soldiers and as fit as could be, but our instructors soon made us think otherwise. Just one hour of training on foot, on the first morning, was enough to make me feel as stiff as a board, which of course didn't make the cross-country run we did immediately afterwards any easier. The sergeant-major is quite something; I've never seen someone of his size, nor heard such a voice. He stands six foot four inches and is nearly as wide as he is tall; his voice reminds me of the air-raid sirens in Paris. At close quarters, all this adds up to a truly terrifying vision, even though he does call us 'Gentlemen'. Now we are allowed to be addressed as such, of course, even though only last week we were called many other names!

My fellow cadets are an interesting motley crew. There are experienced soldiers (that is to say career soldiers, but under twenty-six years old), students, and people who are well known in the world of finance and literature. One is a well-known banker (very young, twenty-nine years old); another is an editor at the *Manchester Guardian*, and so on. Almost everyone has been in the ranks and they have come from every part of England and from every regiment, except for a few students who are in the fast stream and have come directly from university; I feel sure they will bitterly regret this before the end of their career, unless they are extraordinarily talented.

I shall have to work very hard to do well among such company, and indeed I have already started to do so. I have rented a room for £10 for the next five months so that I can work in peace in the evenings. But I am also intending to have some fun and to do some sport in the evenings, which will not only be nice but essential.

That's all for today—not really a letter, but simply a quick note about my first impressions. I shall write more fully next week once I have got used to this place.

With much love from your
Lionel.

2 February, 1942

Dearest Mother,

I think I shall spend the rest of this war apologising for not writing to you more frequently. Here at the OCTU, it's not really because I don't have the time but because, by nine o'clock in the evening, when I have finished getting ready for the next day's parade and have done just a little reading, I am usually so tired that without quite knowing how, I find that I have gone to bed. The intensive preparation by our instructors on the day we arrived has not let up. From seven o'clock in the morning until five o'clock at night, with only one hour for lunch, we are put through a whole range of training activities that are both tough and interesting, but tiring even for the most hardened amongst us—the more stamina we have, the more they require of us.

However, it's a very pleasant and stimulating atmosphere as one would expect in a community of people where everyone has decided to give of their best and do everything possible to achieve our common goal.

I have come across several delightful comrades, amongst them an old friend from Gresham's who was in the same class as I and left school the same year. May I inflict on you a few pen portraits?

There are six of us in our room, including my friend. I will start with the eldest: he is a journalist, twenty-eight years old. He is a thoughtful fellow, but charming also, and he's very gracious towards his turbulent young companions; he laughs into his sleeve when my friend talks about modern poetry, because he writes the weekly column in a literary magazine;

he's very indulgent with me when I climb onto my soapbox and start talking about how the world will be organised in the future; he would have been elected to Parliament had the war not stopped him from standing for election for a second time.

The second had to leave school quite early (for financial reasons). Within a very short time, he had found a good job in a large oil company; he will be a tremendous officer; I like him and my friend from Gresham's the best.

The third one enlisted after two years at university, as he was able to defer his studies; he would have carried on serving in the ranks as a sergeant, but his colonel happened to find out who he was and made him apply to be an officer cadet.

The last one is by far the least interesting; he has come straight from Cambridge under the scheme to fast-track officers, and although he is very bright, in my opinion he's rather lacking in character; I think it will be very good for him to have a bit of a tough time for a few months.

I know my roommates thoroughly, and vice versa; I know the two dozen who are in my group quite well; nearly all the others are complete strangers. I suppose this proves how little free time we have. 'And you'll have even less when you're officers,' we are told by way of encouragement by those in charge. It seems my friend the sergeant was not such a fool after all!

Enough about me and my activities. I wonder how you all are? I heard from Claude that you have found a house to rent and I am delighted. It will be a lot of work to start with, but I know how much you dislike living in a hotel.

Without wishing to probe too deeply, I would love to ask you a few questions, particularly about your financial situation and that of parrain's children who are still in occupied France. I would hate to think you and they are short of anything, while here I have quite a lot of money that I don't really need. Has parrain had any news of his children? V. writes to me from time to time (did you know she has just had a son?). She seems fairly depressed by the lack of news from her parents. Nevertheless she is being very brave, and her life will be quite hard once Philip goes abroad.

With lots and lots of love.

Your Lionel.

12 April, 1942

Dearest Mother,

Thank you very much for your letters. After a long interval, they have finally started to arrive regularly.

I was very sorry to hear you have been so unwell, and especially to learn that I was in some way responsible. You really must not fret about me.

Here, my one concern is to start taking a more active part in the war so we can not only regain the good things of the world we knew, but also start to enjoy the things we have dreamed of in the world to come. I'm becoming more and more used to military life. It's about time! I don't smoke a pipe and I drink very little milk, but I am nevertheless in excellent health and very fit. For the last fifteen months, since I joined the army, apart from one or two small accidents I have not been ill at all.

I could no doubt carry on writing in this vein for a few more pages, and then I would get to the end of the letter without having told you what you really must know; something about which I have been hesitating to write to you for ten days.

You know of course that I have spent the last twelve weeks at the OCTU, and that I was due to leave in about six weeks. Unfortunately, however, that day has been put back yet again. The standards they require of us are very high, too high for me, at least for now. It gives me scant comfort that out of a company of 180 students, all of whom were placed at the top of the list at the time of the selection board and entrance exams, more than fifty of us have been put back. Last Sunday, the colonel called me and told me he had noticed from my file that I had been a non-commissioned officer for very little time (less than three weeks). He said he thought it was essential experience and he would send me back to my regiment as a corporal for a period of three months, after which I should have to restart the officer cadet training from the beginning.

I'm very disappointed. It's the first failure of my life. I know I am far more fortunate than many of my friends (more than thirty since the beginning of the course) who have not been allowed to re-apply, but that's not much of a consolation. The worst thing, for my friends and for me, is that we have worked so hard these last few months! I wrote to you about some of the things that we were doing, and now we have to do it all over again! Five and three makes eight, and I have already done more than a year; at this rate, I should have gone to Saint-Cyr[54] and made a career out of the army!

When you reply to this letter, if you can please avoid referring to what I have just written. I'd just like to know you're not too disappointed, and that you understand I have done my best and will succeed next time around.

Lots of love to you and parrain.

Lionel.

---

[54] The elite officer training college for the French army.

2 June, 1942

Dearest Mother,

Thank you so much for your letter of 28 April. The worst thing about it all was the thought of your disappointment and also that you might have considered it strange I did not succeed at the first attempt, unlike Veronica's husband and his two friends for example. You have put my mind at rest. I'm both pleased and grateful you have accepted this delay without either criticising or advising (both of which would have been so easy), but also without losing confidence in me.

I shall go back to OCTU about the end of August, this time to train specifically for my regiment and two other armoured regiments. For the moment, military life for me is more comfortable than it has ever been. We are in a large and well-equipped camp; everyone has a bed, there is running water in each hut, a good gymnasium and a swimming pool. There is also an hourly bus service into the nearest town; it's a life fit for a king.

I have been put in charge of a platoon of motorcyclists; the training, which is extremely interesting, will last another two months. I now know the name of practically every screw in a motorcycle, so at last I understand how and why 'it works'. As in all the other services, some subjects are interesting and others are tedious, but our training is ample compensation for the chores of administration and organisation.

Most of the chaps in my section were professional couriers before joining up, so they drive brilliantly, as well as the instructors, and they are excellent mechanics. We all get on famously. They know that in some ways they are far more skilled than I am. However, I make it clear that I am happy to acknowledge this, and as a result I'm quite prepared to let them take some of their own decisions, so during training and manoeuvres both on foot and on motorbikes they are happy to accept my orders. The whole British Army understood the value of this 'etiquette' some time ago and has accepted it with good grace.

I have quite a bit of free time. Usually, we only have two night-time manoeuvres per week, and on other days we finish at about 5.30 p.m. During the day we do much less physical training than the infantry. Each week we do two forced marches of about seventeen kilometres, three hours of physical exercise and two hours of weapons training. This seems to be quite sufficient and I am extremely well. I have just won a 200m race, and came second in the 400m and the 100m in our battalion competition. With my prizes (vouchers for the camp shop), I shall be able to give myself indigestion for weeks to come; in one afternoon I won nearly a whole month's pay, and compliments from the colonel!

For some time now I have entertained the idea that I might soon be able to visit you, or that you might be able to come over to Europe. Things seem to be going well; I was on manoeuvres the night 1100 planes bombed Cologne and I saw a very small number of them fly over—it was very impressive! There is a growing sense of strength around me. You might accuse me of being chauvinist—though I don't know if this applies since I'm French—but I'm quite convinced that the British Army is currently the best in the world. The British soldier is better trained than those in any other force fighting in the four corners of the globe. It is hardly fair to blame British soldiers for the way they were handicapped at the start of the war by errors made by the administration, which has anyway since been reorganised. And when our turn comes... then I of all people shall not need to comment.

Do you have any news of Renée? I hope life is not too hard for her. I shall go and see V. when I next have leave. Recently, she has been able to communicate more frequently with her family, so I hope that I shall be able to give you news from France. Mr Oliver Harvey's son is in the same company as I and we shall go to officer cadet training together. He has invited me to his home for a few days. It will be interesting and amusing to see his father again in a very different setting.

With lots of love,

Lionel.

18 June, 1942

Dearest Mother,

I'm writing to you from the most charming setting, sitting comfortably on a reclining deck-chair, and wearing my swimming trunks. It is hot, but not too hot, and I am on my own next to a modern swimming pool full of crystal-clear water.

The day before yesterday I was told that there is a place for me at the OCTU for my regiment, sooner than expected. My course starts on 22 June, which is why I am on leave again nearly five weeks before I was due to be. I am elated. I spent one day in London with Mr d'Erlanger and have now come to stay in a delightful little country hotel next door to V. Her son is a fine specimen. He takes up a lot of her time. She is feeding him herself and never has more than three hours free at a stretch. I managed to take her out dancing yesterday, and we shall play tennis this afternoon. I'm going back to London on Saturday morning and am so pleased to have met up with her again. She is still as charming and pleasant as ever. That's all the news that I have for you from here, except that her husband Philip went abroad with his regiment two months ago, and his first letter has arrived. V. is overjoyed. When I get back to London, I shall go out on the town with Robert Marjolin. [A future member of the Common Market Commission]. Over the weekend I shall also visit Mr Oliver Harvey; his son is also on leave and we start at OCTU together.

On my way from camp to London, a remarkable thing happened. The train had just stopped and I climbed into a first-class compartment that was not full (the rest of the train was crammed). I was just taking off all my equipment and trying to find space for it above the heads and under the legs of the other passengers when I had a very odd sensation. It felt as though all my nerves and senses were suddenly on alert. Without quite knowing why, I turned round and saw, in the opposite corner, your handbag. You know, the big red-orange one – crocodile skin, I think. I was still standing there astonished when a woman dressed in clothes such as you might have worn walked in; both her silhouette and her hair colour were similar to yours. It was only when I saw her face that I was sure that it wasn't you. I never hoped against hope and logic as much as I did during those few seconds. An inkling of how I was feeling must have shown in my face. It was the lady's turn to be concerned. She asked me, 'Is anything wrong?' I answered, 'No, it's nothing, it's not your fault.' Throughout the rest of the journey, there was complete silence. Most of the passengers were wondering, no doubt, how I had managed to escape the attention of the military doctor.

I shall write again soon. All my love,

Lionel.

3 August, 1942

Dearest Mother,

I expect that Mr Grand gave you news of me. I hope you found it to be satisfactory. I am now an officer cadet at the training unit for armoured vehicles, which means that when I pass out I shall either be in my own regiment, the 60th Rifles, or else in the Rifle Brigade if their need is greater. It doesn't really matter, since these two corps are more or less equivalent, and well ahead of all the other regiments.

I'm delighted to hear that Vera Korène is in America. When you see her, please tell her that she has a keen admirer in England, who sends every wish for her success.

How I love you, Mother, and how I love your letters! I read the last one so many times I know it by heart now; you have a greater gift than anyone else for expressing all your personality on paper, and these few pages show me a more real and living picture of you than I have of the friends right here, jostling me and bumping into me. But that is not all; you also managed to remind me so evocatively of my last few happy months in Paris which I hope to relive some day soon. I often think of parrain; I am more than ever influenced by his ideas and his democratic and liberal ideals. Mr d'Erlanger and Mr Marjolin have managed to get hold of several of parrain's talks and lectures for me. In my humble opinion, his talk on the death of Briand is absolutely first-class in every way, as is the one on the rebuilding of Europe—far more interesting, up-to-date and lucid than the ones Mr Ford has delivered. I do hope that the American censors will not stop this letter!!

There are six Americans here with us at the training unit who want to become liaison officers. They are all charming and have managed to stay true to themselves, all the while fitting in. We also have in my section the son of Mosley: he is a first-class chap and very popular (he himself, not his father). I have written already about Harvey's son. There is also an old school friend here who left Gresham's a year before me, and who has managed in very little time to gain a good reputation as an advertisement artist. In his free time, he is writing the history of Impressionism. Even under Mr Newell's enlightened regime, he must have been very bored at school. Incidentally, once again I have spent some truly pleasant days with Mr Newell, who still treats me as if I were one of his pupils, and Mrs Newell continues to look after me like a mother. They are so charming, intelligent and hard working; and so young! It makes me feel enthusiastic and optimistic when I see them, and when I think of you and of Paule and Renée.

I have suddenly realised that Gérard will soon be sixteen. It is good news that you are now a bit more pleased with him; that must mean he's doing well. As for Claude, I have read his poem. It is three years now since I did any literary criticism with Mr Norman, so I will just say I think his English is remarkable—please congratulate him for me.

With lots and lots of love, dearest Mother,

Your Lionel.

10 September, 1942

Dearest Mother,

This time I have been very lucky. Give or take a couple of days, my leave coincided with my birthday and with the debutante ball at Grosvenor House. So I had an extremely suitable party for my twenty-first birthday, a few hours too early but I didn't feel at all guilty about that. I spent the next day, which was Sunday, in a lovely house near London. The only thing missing that weekend was the company that I would most have liked to have had: yours.

I think this present period will probably be one of the happiest of my military life. My friends are delightful, the work is fascinating and I am deriving great benefit from it; best of all—and this may well not happen again—I'm enjoying all these good things without any of the usual attendant difficulties.

It's not easy for me to tell Gérard exactly what I think when comparing his life to mine. Maybe he has changed a lot and is now working a bit harder, and of course I am far from perfect; I know it only too well and ask for forgiveness. I also remember vividly the ways in which I begged you to let me enlist before I was the right age; in all honesty, I do not regret it, but the situation has changed rather. In a year's time, Gérard will still only be seventeen and a half; even now, the English are only calling up young men of nineteen, often allowing students to delay enlisting, and they even send those who have already enlisted to follow university courses for between six months and a year. It seems to me that the experience of university study is absolutely essential.

There will be a great need after a military victory for people of intelligence and good education—the work will only just be starting. And a university education is of the greatest value to a military man.

Modern warfare requires a high level of initiative and intelligence and is increasingly becoming a personal struggle between ever-smaller units under the direct command of junior officers.

At school, the best students are the ones who have already learned how to think, plan, and analyse situations. The advice given me by Mr Norman is even more useful to me now than it was when I was taking exams and had three hours to think about the question, to make a plan—now I'm lucky if I have ten minutes.

And that is not everything: a good military education might possibly produce the same results. But a modern soldier is only in action for very short periods of time, and during inactive periods he needs to keep his spirits up in the fog of boring daily routine. This is when the value of a university education comes into its own. A young man who has studied is better able to keep a grip on himself. He will generally have a clearer idea of the ideal for which he is fighting. The lessons I learned at Sciences Politiques, I think it fair to say, have helped me to avoid making silly mistakes. Lamartine's *Le Lac* and André Chénier's *La Jeune Tarentine* saved me from many hours of depression. The declaration of human rights still inspires me.

The only excuse for war is when it is fought for the sake of an ideal. It is our duty to realise this ideal and bring it about. Anyone who is content, after peace, simply to go home and consider his job done will have committed the greatest crime, for he will have killed for no reason and without trying to make things better. I see once again that I have climbed onto my soapbox—please forgive me. I simply wanted to say to Gérard that he is not yet old enough, either in mind or in body, to enlist in a year's time. I recommend that he should study at university for as long as he can, while at the same time doing some military training or some flying.

I went to see Mr Pleven when I was last in London. I also visited Mr Warren-Low, who asked me if his son was right in saying he preferred to stay a sergeant because the conversation in his mess seemed more interesting than that in the officers mess. Do you see much of Mrs d'Erlanger? Her husband has been so kind; I don't know what I would have done without him. Is parrain intending to come here one day soon? From a purely objective point of view, I recommend it highly. And you really must come over—we have not seen each other for such a long time! Surely that is the best of excuses?

A thousand kisses.

Lionel.

4 December, 1942

Dearest Mother,

I have been back at camp for nearly a week now after a month of battle training. I am not revealing any military secrets if I tell you that the training and tactics we have been learning are those which enabled Montgomery to win at El Alamein. I don't think I'm being wildly optimistic in claiming that they will enable us to beat the Germans in the future wherever we find them. We were tired when we got back after a week of forced marches through countryside and mountains, carrying our own blankets as well as our normal battle-kits and rations! It was no rest-cure, but it was very rewarding to discover by the end that both my companions and I were able to survive such an ordeal and, immediately afterwards, to go on the attack in an exercise in which real bullets and real shells were used. In the end, we achieved our objectives as well as if we had been fresh troops! It gave us all tremendous confidence in ourselves and in the training we've received. The only part I found really hard was coming back by night in convoy. I nearly fell asleep on my motorcycle several times, as in the two previous nights I had only had two hours' sleep.

Yesterday we were reviewed by the colonel-in-chief of the regiment and two generals. It was impressive to see the change when our platoons got into their ceremonial uniform rather than battledress. After the parade, we met individually with the colonel-in-chief who read the reports from our instructors and welcomed us into the regiment, which we shall join as officers in the New Year, after going on leave. My report could have been written by you: the same criticisms and the same compliments, though I do seem to have overcome some of my former shortcomings. As I was saluting and saying thank you, I suddenly remembered a series of events, a hypothesis made up of memories: a lovely day spent playing golf at Saint-Cloud, classes at Science Politiques, a mass in Notre Dame, a matinée at the Théâtre Français, and then the nearly deserted streets of Paris through which I walked for the last time with Colette[55] before leaving Paris the next day.

The heavy traffic on the roads, the panic at Bordeaux, the bravery of Paule and Renée as they said goodbye, and then finally at Chicago station, so cold and so hostile, the last picture

---

[55] A good friend from Sciences Politiques.

that I have of you in my mind's eye. So from now on, at last I can say to myself that even if at the moment I'm not involved in any action, it is now down to me to help to direct events instead of simply going along with them. My comrades and I will be making our own futures.

Maybe I am too impulsive? I talk much, but I have done so little! If ever, when I am hungry, cold, in pain, fearful; if at that moment I continue in spite of everything to do my duty, it may be because I will remember having written this letter and the reason why I wrote it.

I have not had any news of my brothers for quite some time. Is Gérard still going to enlist, and what did he think of my advice? I would very much like to know what he is planning to do. I am not at all worried about Claude, he will gain confidence and find his own way quite quickly. Please just make sure that he learns, from now on, how to have fun and be happy.

And you, dearest Mother, how are you? Please do not worry about me. My tailor has made a superb uniform, and I promise you'll see me wearing it without any holes or tears. I dream of eating one of your steaks, not only because I am so greedy that I often dream about steaks, but also because I know that you would prepare it exactly as I like it.

With lots and lots of love.

Lionel

PART 3

An officer in England and in Egypt

LIONEL HAD FINALLY BEEN COMMISSIONED as lieutenant, his goal for the last twenty months, and was now faced with the new responsibilities of which he was keenly aware.

He was particularly proud to be put in charge of a motorised platoon in the 10th battalion of the King's Royal Rifle Corps, one of the most distinguished British regiments and one that had been home to some of the most famous names in the United Kingdom. The regiment in the British Army is not only a military and administrative unit; it is also, in some ways, a club. Sir Ronald Campbell was an envoy and an adviser at the British Embassy in Washington, and when I told him which unit Lionel had been promoted into he exclaimed with great pleasure and pride, 'Oh, I'm so pleased to hear that! The KRRC is my own family regiment.'

Lionel's letters from this time are full of lively and amusing observations on the unwritten yet extremely important rules governing the life of a young officer. The secret of life in Britain is that it requires one to very carefully, at all times and in all circumstances, observe the rules of the game... and Lionel enjoyed describing this.

For four months, Lionel was given special training in driving and maintaining vehicles; in chemical warfare and in battle manoeuvres. At the end of spring his unit embarked for Cairo, the headquarters of the forces in the Middle East. Before leaving, he wrote his will and put all his affairs in order.

The crossing lasted about two months. He arrived in Egypt at the end of June, and remained for about five months, not far from Cairo.

During those five months, his unit was training in the desert using vehicles and light tanks. Lionel loved this active life under a harsh sun. He was particularly delighted to be back in his childhood home. Friends and relatives were pleased and proud to see him and welcomed him warmly. Dr Grossi, the doctor who had cared for him as a child, said to me a few weeks ago, 'Lionel came to see me; as he spoke about the issues that would need to be faced after the war, his eyes lit up and he almost seemed to have a halo.'

The happiest hours during his time in Egypt were those he spent with his former nurse, Sophie, whom he called Nani. She had married his father's chauffeur, Benjamin, who had been brought up by Jacques Mosséri. By this time he had opened a garage. Lionel's camp was about a hundred kilometres from Cairo. When he was free in the evenings, he liked to come into town to have supper and spend time with his friends. If it was too late to find a taxi, Benjamin drove him back to camp. Sometimes Benjamin lent him a car and, if it broke down in the desert, it was Benjamin who came to repair it. When Lionel spent the weekend in Cairo, he usually stayed with Nani. 'What would you like for breakfast tomorrow?'—'A steak.' Benjamin would run out to buy the steak and Sophie would cook it. Both refused any kind of the payment for this simple yet generous hospitality.It was in Cairo that Lionel had a particularly idyllic experience, which I shall mention further on.

12 January, 1943

Dearest Mother,

I rejoined my battalion five days ago after a week's leave.

I had feelings similar to those on the day I first enlisted: I was given the same equipment and sleeping bag; once again there were many good resolutions. There was something of the mix of excitement, fear and regret I experienced on platform 9 for the 2:30 p.m. train back to Gresham's after the holidays.

Life in England is a succession of more or less regular scenarios, as a game of bridge, played more or less with the same cards and the same players. From an objective point of view, the stakes are increasingly important, but one always experiences the immediate present as the most important: preparatory school, public school, university, army, club, civil service. You only need to learn the rules once—it really is that simple—and I can see why there is a strong reluctance to introduce foreigners into the game who do not understand how to play the game.

There was a pleasant surprise when I got to the station. My batman was somebody I had trained with as a new recruit, and with whom I had always got on very well. And there was another bit of good news: my commanding officer was someone under whom I had served for six weeks as corporal before going to OCTU.

On the minus side, I have been absorbed into the workings of a gigantic machine powered by centuries of tradition. I went to visit the colonel and signed my confidential reports (they could have been written by you and by Mr Newell), and heard the traditional sermon which had the desired if paradoxical result of convincing me that it is my function and not my person that is all-important. We then dined in the mess.

I shall never forget that dinner. Everyone was in dress uniform—not only their clothes, but their manners as well. There were famous people present: the man who had led the last expedition up Everest, members of old families, the chancellor of a major university, some young lieutenants who had been all over the papers because of their military exploits...The whole event was conducted in almost complete silence, broken only from time to time by a question from a superior officer and the very short and to-the-point answer from a subordinate officer. The oddest thing –yes, it really is me writing this—is that I felt extremely honoured when asked to pass the salt!

And yet that very morning, the same officers had nearly all been covered in oil, dust or sweat, had slept outside under a simple blanket and waterproof sheet with their men. It was a very impressive contrast. In the company mess, where there are only a few officers, the rules are of course much more relaxed and I have already met a couple of chaps I like very much.

Tomorrow I shall take over my men, my equipment, my four lorries and my motorbike. It is now 3 a.m.; I have spent the night reading the reports on each of my men (written by their previous officer), and putting together filing cards with their characteristics.

I seem to have a bit of everything. One is a member of a symphony orchestra and one a jazz player; I have entrepreneurs, professional football players who were earning more than I ever shall, a boxer, a professional motorcycle rider, and one man who has spent nearly half his life in prison. Between them they make up a splendid unit: I hope they will love and trust me. I am amazed

by the number of people whose only wish is to live in peace—
and I do mean live, not exist. They want to have a family
and children, to educate themselves, to be constructive, and
not overwhelmed by desires or ambitions. This seems almost
unbelievable, given the storm we are all in the midst of. These
men have wives and children and they are ready to sacrifice
everything in order to ensure the kind of life they want. I will
do my very best to bring as many as possible home safe and
sound. There must inevitably be losses, but we must ensure
that these are not in vain. And yet, as I write, evil monsters are
plotting and setting up future discord. Please remind parrain
of the promise he made before I left.[56]

I saw Claire recently. I am well aware that she is a fine
person and a fine woman, but that doesn't seem to be a reason
for her to treat me as if I were still sixteen. She has been my
Roxane for a long time, but it would be lovely to move beyond
the first few lines of the balcony scene.[57]

I'm becoming very sleepy now. Goodnight, dearest mother,
please write soon.

With all my love,
Lionel.

10th Battalion, the King's Royal Rifle Corps
20 February, 1943

Dearest Mother,

I have just spent a very pleasant fortnight at the seaside, at
a kind of health spa visited by people in peace-time who are
suffering from imaginary illnesses. They undergo painless

---

[56] To take Lionel on as a secretary.
[57] Reference to Edmond Rostand's Cyrano de Bergerac: in the balcony scene,
Roxane initially treats the amorous Christian with disdain, but as the scene
progresses she is won over by eloquence.

cures while staying in delightful little huts between a private beach on the seaward side and large private grounds on the landward side. It is not peace-time now, I am not suffering from any imaginary illnesses, and the Army is not looking for painless cures. So why did I go there?

I myself was very surprised to be selected for this special physical education course, and once again most surprised to find myself in such a pleasant place.

The mess is quite a modern house with all modern comforts—hot and cold baths—and extremely well furnished. The training programme and the atmosphere were both very relaxed—not at all characteristic of the Army. We trained between 9 a.m. and 12:30 p.m. and between 2 p.m. and 4:30 p.m., just wearing fatigues: boots, trousers and a pullover. After ten months of battle training, I felt almost naked.

The fortnight passed too quickly. We had only two hours a day of physical education proper. The rest of the time we swam in the sea, boxed, wrestled, and did 'road work' and cross-country running. I was pretty fit before we started, so I was able to enjoy every moment and was delighted to have wangled such a pleasant stay. However, I was brought back down to earth when I got back to camp and the officer in charge said he was counting on me to organise a similar camp for my battalion. That may sound good, but I'm only too well aware that it is a big challenge. I shall need to find a place for it; accommodation, instructors, equipment. Schedules, reports, record cards, and a filing system will be required… why in heaven's name can't they send me abroad soon?

Slowly but surely I'm developing a deep hatred of military administration. When I left OCTU, I thought that from then on I would be supervising individual training and drawing up tactical plans. What an incurable optimist I am! I do have to do those things, but that's only a very small part of the bigger picture. On paper at least, I am supposed to have a lot of free time, but I have to go to meetings, set timetables, maintain records and write letters.

One of the men in my platoon is going to become a father and wants to know what I can do to obtain help for his wife. At this very moment, I know enough about the needs of babies before and after their arrival to write a whole book on the subject.

And then there is the corporal who, I promise you, could meet ten Germans without blinking and yet came to see me, distressed and upset, to show me an anonymous letter he had just received—it was the same old story: the husband was the last to know. I told him he was silly to have read it and promised to try to get him sent on leave. I also had to write to the wife that, as the officer commanding his platoon, I was in a good position to appreciate her husband's value both to the army and to society, and I was sure she would not want the burden of knowing that she had slackened her war effort by breaking off her relationship with him while he was carrying out the highest duty of any Englishman—three years of happiness, etc., etc.; and I was counting on her to put an end to any rumours that might be distressing her husband. I have not yet received any answer but when it comes, it will either be amusing and unsatisfying, or simply satisfying. In either case, my corporal will not know I have written to her.

The post has been very bad recently. I did not know anything about your operation until after it had happened.

Please don't tell me it is just as well. It is your letters above all, and the news they bring, that I long for most—except of course the joy of being with you again.

I fear it will be very difficult for you to telephone me, because you can only reach me during my leave periods. As soon as I have a definite date for my next leave I will send you a cable giving the dates.

Do you have any news from France? V.'s sister has just arrived from Algiers and I hope to see her soon. How are Gérard and Claude?

I would love to hear news of Denyse and Vera Korène. I promise I will reply to them.

I will write again soon, dearest Mother.

With lots and lots of love,

Lionel.

10 Bn. The KRRC.

6 March, 1943

Dearest Mother,

A few hours ago this would have been very different letter, so please don't read too much into it. I am in a foul mood, and as I can't say anything to anyone in the mess, and there is no other way of venting my frustration, and because I'm still furious even after having counted to 10 ten times, I will tell you the whole story.

Last week, the colonel happened to be at the camp where I was teaching some junior officers all kinds of mean tricks that can be used if one is disarmed and attacking an enemy who may or may not be disarmed. My men were working well and with much enthusiasm, quite possibly because the colonel was present. When I had finished my class, the great man came over. 'Good work! If you have time, I would be grateful for a half-hour of instruction myself, as I'm a bit rusty.'

So for thirty minutes I refreshed his memory and showed him a number of things that a gentleman is not supposed to know which the Apaches, the Japanese and other undesirables practise with a great deal of success: how to strangle someone on guard, how to parry a knife attack, and other such charming skills.

The colonel is relatively young—thirty-eight years old—and very strong, and we had a good time. I took my leave of him and continued my job.

This morning, I saw my name on the list of instructors. This means that instead of leading my little group and having a good chance of going abroad with my own men in the near future, I will have to stay in England for another three to six months. I had been so much hoping to leave soon! It's really infuriating to have trained for two years just for this.

And of course, I'm very disappointed. It's really no fun being an officer in my regiment. In theory, there are no particular rules, but in practice one has to dine in the mess at eight o'clock nearly every evening, or else questions will be asked.

Everything around here closes at ten, so there is very little opportunity to go out; if a young officer does find an opportunity to return after eleven a few nights running, he had better not appear in the least tired at physical training before breakfast. The men, however, may stay out until midnight, and even in this little backwater they seem to find much more entertainment than we do. Enough. I have just been given an old copy of Pantagruel by a friend, and I'm ashamed to make a fuss when I think of what life is like in France. I almost think I should tear up this letter.

With lots of love,

Lionel.

23 March, 1943

Dearest Mother,

At the moment I am on another course. This time, the training establishment is directly under the Ministry of War, which means the marks we get carry weight and we have to work quite hard. It would be difficult anyway to do otherwise. During the actual training sessions, our instructors are experts at extracting maximum effort from their students. After training, there are very few leisure opportunities.

The school is in a delightful place in the Lake District. They have requisitioned a big hotel, which is very comfortable and quite isolated. The landscape is magical: gentle valleys, with plenty of streams, and wooded hillsides.

There is a sweet little lake that ingratiatingly, slowly and gently continuously licks and kisses the lower slopes of a great hill, to no avail, as the hill remains impassively and coldly still, and does not even bother repelling these timid, fond advances. The few local residents are very hospitable.

Last Sunday, I went for a wonderful hike with a friend. A poster outside a little cottage caught our attention and we went in. The clock was put back two years and we had a real English tea. Eggs (yes, two each), bacon, toasted scones with strawberry jam, and a real fruitcake to finish with. How, why? We didn't try to understand this mystery. It was all very modestly priced.

Maybe there are still, even in England, a few peaceful little places where 'war' is only a word and life goes on as it always has done, following the rhythm of nature and untroubled by man-made cataclysms. Was I wrong to find it so refreshing, so encouraging?

This war is a total war: the rights of any single person are uncertain, even the right to life. Would anyone dare to say that it is nothing to do with them, that they wash their hands of the whole matter? I don't think this is the issue.

To me, this little cottage on the hillside was not an artificial ivory tower but a symbol, both a promise for the future and a memory of the past. My friend said, 'I shall come back,' and I said, 'I won't.'

The training is interesting, but it's even more interesting to meet so many different people. We are only together for three weeks, so most of the protocol and reserve of a battalion mess are simply not present. For a very short time, this is really nice.

Yesterday, I listened to Churchill's speech. I felt this might be the most important moment of my life – as though I had been present at the Declaration of the Rights of Man in 1789.

Three years into the war, we finally have a positive reason to fight; before it was simply what we had to. I felt that I would only be able to start fighting for my ideas and my convictions after the war, but now I find that there is a man able to realise these ideas, a man chosen freely by a great and powerful nation; a man who, knowing all the facts, is able to set them out rationally and make splendid plans to implement them. I was suddenly overcome with gratitude and whispered, 'Thank you!'

With lots of love,
Lionel

(Original letter in English)
(At sea)

2 June, 1943

Dearest Mother,

I hope you were not worried when my telegram of 10 April reached you. I was not allowed to tell you that I was about to leave England. Even now I'm not allowed to tell you where I am going.

During my last leave, I went again to see Mr Newell, and spent the rest of my time in London with Mr d'Erlanger. All my papers, my will and my accounts are in his bank and, it so happens, in good order. I have arranged for Gérard to be able to draw on my funds if he comes to enlist in England.[58]

I do hope that in the meantime we shall have been able to polish everything off without him. Please don't let him enlist unless he has to, as he will be much more useful in his university.

For the first time for nearly three years, I'm starting to plan again for the future. Unfortunately, it seems you may not be able to return to France immediately after the end of the war, because of the work that parrain is doing to prepare for peace. As soon as I am released from the army, I would like to return

---

[58] Gérard was very keen to serve in the air force. The French military mission in Washington told him that he had very little chance of becoming a pilot. Several months later, however, he was able to enlist in the naval air forces.

to higher education. Not only am I more and more convinced that my life will be closely identified with study, but also, on a practical level, it is a very good investment, and it is also a very good way of spending the two years immediately after the war which are likely to be quite troubled. And afterwards? Even now, I don't dare look any further ahead.

Please write long letters, dearest Mother, as your letters are now my only reason for living. Do you remember a letter I wrote during my last term at Gresham's, in which I said I was so pleased that soon I would no longer have to write to say how much I loved you?

This sea voyage is very pleasant. I am sharing a cabin with an officer of the field security police. He is a very interesting fellow. He was at a good school until he was eighteen, and then suddenly decided that was not the life for him, so he left his family and became, first, a porter in a second-rate hotel, then a greengrocer, then a soldier in an overseas regiment. Just before the war, he published two books which are selling quite well.

On this ship there is also an air force colonel, quite young, who was a flying ace in the Battle of Britain. He is also one of the most charming people I have ever met. Yesterday, we were watching seagulls when he suddenly exclaimed, 'That silly bird is flying too low, it's going to crash', and that is exactly what happened. I loved the idea of teaching birds to fly!

Yesterday evening, we had a lecture from a captain who was commanding a destroyer at the Battle of Narvik in April 1940. He talked about that battle and the Norwegian campaign in general. He had a natural and calm manner. On the whole, I think I prefer the army. I have quite a lot to do, organising training for my men, and of course I have to do a lot myself. The rest of the time is taken up with fitness training, discussions, plays, concerts, etc. Life is not too dull. At the beginning of the voyage, a number of the young officers were excited that we were taking with us a cargo of nurses and WAAFS. They soon got over it: I have never seen such a collection of unattractive women; as we go we shall gradually lose them ...

With love from

Lionel.

No. 2 I.TD.
KRRC
M.E.F.

15 July, 1943

Dearest Mother,

It is about a fortnight since we reached this new camp. In case you did not receive my other letters, let me reiterate that it was a fairly good voyage—fairly good because it was both long and boring, and also because, as army officers, we had very little authority so it was not easy to make life as pleasant on board for our men as we would have liked.

Now I am settled at this camp. It could have been worse: we are in the middle of the desert, about a hundred kilometres from Cairo, but everything is very well organised. It's not quite the same as life at Ghezireh[59]—malesh![60] I hope this is the final staging-post. We have just completed our first routine training—desert marching, navigation, and so on—and I shall be going off soon to a specialist training facility, after which I hope to take command of a unit of tankettes. They are the best

[59] The part of Cairo where the family lived during Lionel's childhood.
[60] Arabic word meaning 'no matter'.

and the most interesting of the armoured vehicle battalion, so I really hope I shall do well enough to qualify. I have been to visit the family, but I'm not able to do so very often. I've also been to see Mr Perez and Mrs Sacopoulo, and of course Nani. Everyone has been so very kind, but I had a feeling—goodness knows why—that they all expected me, as the son of a widow given a liberal education, to have become a dissolute young man. God bless you, dearest Mother, and thank you so much for your discipline. I think they were a bit disappointed to see that I neither smoke nor drink—they were longing to exercise tolerance! But no, I must be fair—they were really good to me.

As for Nani, how did I deserve the deep fondness she has for me? It would have been embarrassing not to display some emotion. After the war, we must have her back with us.

Do send me a wire to say what you are going to do about Gerard. I think he will find it hard to join the RAF now, as they are up to their full complement and most of those taken on as pilots have been in training for two years before joining up. If he wants to join the army, he could easily come into my regiment, which is after all playing a major role in this war. Otherwise I fear he may be sent into some other African battalion. Does he absolutely have to join up? As an engineering student, he should be entitled to deferment, and in all honesty, at this point in the war I think he would be of much more use at his university.

Things are going very well for us, and this is only the start. The British Army has been training furiously, following the methods of Alexander and Montgomery, for two years, and it has not yet shown its full potential: when the moment comes, the Germans are going to cop it!

One morning I found five puppies in my tent. The bitch is very sweet but not very attentive, and she has already started to flirt with another dog in the camp, so I have adopted the puppies and she seems very grateful. They take up a lot of my spare time.

I will write again soon, dearest Mother.

With lots of love from

Lionel.

5 Coy No. 2 J.T.D.

KRRC

26 August 1943

Dearest Mother,

After a month of intensive training, I have just had a week's leave in Cairo, which I really needed. The training itself is not very different from what we had in England, but the temperature here is not at all the same.

On the first day, we did an exercise in the desert, about fifteen kilometres away from the camp, leaving by lorry. Once we had finished, the instructors decided to make us hike back at a clip. In England, I was no longer worried by physical endurance exercises, as I knew I could hold out as long as anyone else, but this time I must admit I was a bit concerned. There are pleasanter pastimes than running fifteen kilometres in the desert at midday. As all our instructors were members of the Eighth Army, [formed in September 1941 from the British Commonwealth army formation known as the Western Desert Force], I wasn't sure I could say to myself, as I usually do,

'If they can do it, then so can I!' After three kilometres I was sweating profusely, and my thoughts about the army at that stage would have had me court-martialled had I voiced them aloud. The sergeant running beside me, a cockney, was also extremely fed up: '*** army, I joined up to come and fight, not to become a *** long-distance Olympic champion!' He was so cheeky I was tempted to laugh, but didn't want to waste my breath. My wretched kit was really awkward, and I just wanted to throw it to the ground and myself along with it. I couldn't show myself to be more tired than my comrades, but when would the darned instructors have had enough of this? Suddenly, behind a dune, we saw our lorries and our instructors, and they were laughing at us: 'You didn't really think we'd make you go all the way back to camp at this rate?' They had truly taken us in, and once we'd calmed down we joined in the joke. Maybe it'll be our turn one day.

The training went well, and I learned a few things that it would be costly not to know in action.

I spent the first day of my leave at Ismailiah, where there were regattas. In the evening, I ate at the Cercle Français, where most of the longer-serving members are employees of the Suez Canal Company. I introduced myself to a naval lieutenant-commander and his wife, who invited me to join their table. They were very kind, but about halfway through the meal, the lady skilfully led up to asking why I was in the British Army. This led on, even here, to the usual petty discussions and narrow views, and the sterile and circular debates about 'de Gaulle or Giraud'![61] I really was not prepared to put up with it, 'Madame, when I left France in 1940 and joined up as a private in England, there was only one issue—to fight the Germans.'

---

[61] General Giraud was involved in an uneasy alliance with de Gaulle. He was inclined to work closely with the United States, of whom de Gaulle was wary.

She said nothing further about it. I have been invited to go and visit them whenever I can next time I am on leave.

With lots of love from

Lionel.

5 Coy—3 Bn KRRC

B.M.E.F.

20 October, 1943

Dearest Mother,

For officers, life at camp generally consists of periods of intense training followed by periods of boring routine work.

This time, I didn't have any particular training to do, and my commanding officer thought his men had reached a sufficient level and could do with a few days' rest. Of course, not everyone could go on leave, and even if they had been able to, most would have turned the offer down. Many have not taken any leave for a while now, because they know that in Cairo or Alexandria they would quickly run through all their savings.

Our commanding officer decided to requisition some lorries and send his men off into the desert for a three-day expedition, equipped with all the rations they would need. Their only duty would be to take turns driving on a variety of difficult terrains. It was a very good idea, and it worked perfectly.

To add to our rations, I bought eggs, tomatoes, some preserves and fruits, and we set off. The temperature in the desert is very pleasant now—it's not as hostile as it was in the summer. The sand is no longer white-hot and soft, but gently undulating and alive with a whole range of delicately coloured shadows. The sun is still hot, but there is usually a gentle breeze; it is indescribably sweet to stand, naked from the waist up, on a lorry travelling fast across the infinitely wide plain of blues and yellows. It's impossible to relive the feeling when sitting at a table: it's too vague and escapes the imagination—it simply cannot be set down in black symbols on white paper.

Driving for eight hours a day still leaves a lot of time for sunbathing and organising games. We had a good supper in the evening—it's amazing what you can put together on a little oil stove in the sand – and anyone who was not too tired would stay up and exchange stories.

One of my men described an attack by German tanks on his position in Tunisia. As he is a cockney, he can't help being amusing, and he started his tale in an even, unremarkable tone: 'It was a beautiful night, sir, and the soldiers were lying dreaming under the stars, while the officers dreamed they were lying on the stars.' General hilarity. So he carried on with his story with great satisfaction.

One corporal always has his trumpet—it's been with him in the desert for three years, so it's seen quite a few campaigns. He plays 'Tristesse' and the ballad 'I'll walk beside you through the night'. Then he quickly changes the mood from serious to light and starts playing jazz.

After this, conversation tends to become more general. I caught bits and pieces of it: beer, cinema, girlfriends, motorbikes... but not the things they really care about: family, wives, children, their home and sitting by the fire.

Every time I get a few moments alone with one of my chaps I wonder why Stuart Mill was wrong when he said he had so much faith in the innate kindness and good sense of people that, if everyone could read and were able to, and if all opinions were freely exchanged, all economic and social problems would automatically be solved. Original sin. Faust—who can tell?

I am delighted to hear that parrain, Gérard and Claude are well. Please continue to look after them, and spare a thought for me. I love you all very, very much.

Lionel.

See opposite page
[62] He joined the Raiding Support Regiment, a kind of super commando group made up only of volunteers, and under the command of Lieutenant-Colonel Sir Thomas Devitt. There is a letter from him in the Appendix. The remarks by Sir Thomas are confirmed by the following report, received from Colonel Molloy, the British military attaché in Washington: 'In November 1943, Lionel Mosséri joined the Raiding Support Regiment and was involved in raids across the desert area against enemy lines of communication, and against important points of resistance behind enemy lines.'

PART 4

Palestine, Italy, Yugoslavia

FOR A FEW MONTHS, Lionel had been leading a tankette unit. He feared this would not give him all the opportunities he craved to meet Germans face to face, so he asked to be transferred to a special service unit in the Raiding Support Regiment.

In the first few days of November 1943 he was granted his wish, and left Egypt for Palestine, where he started to train in parachute jumping—a particular trial for him as he was very prone to nose-bleeds.[62]

After three months of special operations, Lionel was put in charge of a small unit of machine-guns (Vickers), and left Palestine to go to Italy and join another regiment of the Raiding Forces in a small rural village.

He was involved in action almost immediately. For about three months, from March to June, he took part in more or less continuous operations in Italy and Yugoslavia, and threw himself into them with confidence and enthusiasm. Finally, after what had seemed to him an interminable period of waiting, he was able to deploy against the enemy the stamina, the technical knowledge and the leadership skills he had been accumulating during three years of preparation and intensive training. He was at last able to take a direct and active part in the war, and moreover in operations that were extremely daring and required all his bravery. This period, together with the six weeks he spent fighting in France, was the most interesting and fulfilling of his military career. It was also the most illustrious: at the age of twenty-two, only eighteen months after his commission, he was promoted to captain and gained the DSO,[63] rarely awarded to young officers.

No doubt the reader would be interested to know much about Lionel's life during this particularly active phase of his military career. Unfortunately it is almost impossible to piece together the history of this campaign. The reasons for the paucity of evidence are easy to understand.

There are few letters from Lionel. He neither had the time to write, nor any way of posting letters when operating behind enemy lines—he was careful to alert his mother to the fact that he might not be able to write for prolonged periods.

The missions he was engaged in were all highly secret. He was careful to observe the strict regulations about discretion in military correspondence.

I recently made close enquiries from the British Ministry of War, and was told that regrettably the information I was requesting was not available, as they themselves did not have detailed reports of the military operations Lionel had been involved in during this period.

The parachute units to which he belonged were not attached to his original regiment. They were constantly being reshaped to make up for heavy losses, and were often made up of rather disparate elements in order to create confusion among the enemy as to the characteristics of the units they were facing. Once they were in enemy territory, they operated on an almost individual basis.[64]

---

[63] Distinguished Service Order.
[64] This explains why his commanding officer, who had a warm regard for Lionel's courage, was not able to recall the details of the operations in which Lionel took part under his command.

The only reports I have are general in nature and give no precise details of the exact geographical locations to which they refer. These reports, both verbal and in writing, were gathered several months after the events themselves.

In a letter dated 15 August 1944, which appears in Part 6, Lionel mentions eleven jumps he made in Yugoslavia in the spring of that year. In a letter of 25 February 1945, his former commanding officer in the 1st group of French commandos, Lieutenant-Colonel Vallon, writes proudly of the experience his guerrilla recruit had acquired in Italy and Yugoslavia.[65] And lastly, the comrades with whom Lionel lived on a daily basis in Algiers between July and September 1944 have been able to pass on a few pithy stories from this particularly testing campaign.[66]

Lionel belonged to those groups of British parachutists who, on a number of occasions, jumped behind enemy lines to support and provision the Yugoslav partisans. The aim was to give space to Marshal Tito, whom the Germans were trying to confine to the Dalmatian coast, and who was in a critical position. The partisans with whom he was cooperating were acting with extreme daring, conducting raids down into the plains from the mountains to attack German convoys and supply lines, giving no quarter—nor did they expect any if they failed.

It was during these raids that Lionel personally witnessed atrocities committed by the Germans of which, several months later, he could only talk with tears in his eyes. After a violent fight, a village was taken from the enemy, and Lionel was among those who went in, going with a Yugoslav who was looking forward to seeing his pregnant wife again. They both

---

[65] See the letter from Lieutenant-Colonel Vallon in the Appendix.
[66] Especially Major Linette Terré, Captain France de la Chaise, Lieutenant Richou and Sergeant Trompette.

hurried towards the house, where they found a dead woman. The Germans had cut open her stomach, replaced the child with a cat, and then sewn up the woman, who was still alive.[67]

Another time, he was shown a row of bodies: all the babies in a particular little hamlet. They had been killed by being tossed, still alive, into the air, and then shot as if they were pigeons.

Having seen these atrocities and many others, Lionel developed a tremendous hatred for the German monsters. He swore he would never spare any, and would kill any that came near him with his own hand.

There were occasional rays of sunshine among the general horror. A small town was retaken, and the partisans organised a local dance to celebrate. Lionel joined in and danced with the local girls. He singled out a particularly fine-looking girl from Dalmatia with dark eyes, who also belonged to a group of partisans and fought with them. It was a wonderful evening, with lively conversation between them. As the night drew on, the girl said to him, 'We've danced enough. Tomorrow we have to go off elsewhere, and we need to sleep now. You won't find a room here, so come and share my tent.' Lionel could not refuse this simple and uncomplicated invitation – uncomplicated because both men and women among the partisans had sworn to keep themselves chaste during their operations, and anyone failing to observe this was to be executed. Lionel spent a bad night, unable to sleep. His pretty companion was lying next to him, with two activated grenades under her pillow in case of a sudden enemy attack. Lionel spent the night worrying that a sudden movement by the girl might set off a grenade. While well prepared to give his life to gain a strategic position or kill an enemy guard, he was reluctant to die a ridiculous death.

[67] Letter from Major L. Terré, 25 January, 1946.

At the beginning of May he was once again in Italy and was particularly grumpy at being turned down for a position he was desperate to obtain.[68] Parachute operations were being planned into the mountains in the southeast of France, timed to coincide with landings on the Provence coast. Lionel applied to join these units so that he could take part. However, he was turned down, as he was considered key to his current unit. He went off to Yugoslavia for a further month, and only then was he allowed to transfer into the unit in which he would be able to fight, as he longed to, on French soil for the liberation of France.[69]

From what I have been able to find out, the centre in which he was appointed as inspector and which trained British and American troops was in Staoueli, near Algiers. An operation was planned, and Lionel was to take part. The plane flew towards France, crossed the coastline and arrived at the point identified for the drop. A few seconds before the jump, a radio message was received to say that the receiving unit had been captured by the Germans, so the plane had to turn round and go back.

It was now too late to plan any further operations ahead of the landings in Provence, so Lionel found himself temporarily inactive. It was at this point that he decided to join the French army.

His letters during this busy time were infrequent, and made only passing reference to the military operations he was engaged in; they are of great interest nevertheless. In his brief moments of respite from danger, he revisited the questions that haunted him concerning the building of peace and of a better world. He was very critical of the Italians, whom he was able to observe

[68] Letter, 2 May, 1944.
[69] Letter, 15 October, 1944.

at close quarters. And he seems to have been increasingly concerned about how the English would behave after the war. He had developed an enormous admiration for Britain and the British army, but he feared that the mood among the British people—which had been strengthened by Dunkirk, and had grown into a steely united front during the Battle of Britain, so far unbroken—would fall apart after victory. He thought the lack of focus, the need to attend to individual needs and the return to normal daily life would distract public opinion from the huge task that lay ahead: the establishment of a lasting peace and improved social conditions.

Letter to Mlle Simone Cattaui
(Original letter in English)

22 December 1943

"A" Bty RSR, Raiding Forces, M.E.F.

My dear Simone,

I heard from D. that your mother is not very well. I would be most grateful if you would send me news of her; I do hope it will be good news.

In her last letter, my mother told me that Gerry has enlisted.[70] I knew, of course, the day would come when he too would leave, but the idea seemed so incredible that I thought it would never actually happen.

Now that it has, I find I am more depressed than I have been since the day I enlisted myself. Simone, he is still only a boy, even more so than I was at his age! It all seems so pointless, especially as the end of the war is in sight, and seems to be

---

[70] His brother Gérard.

irrevocable, mathematically certain, and pitiless. It's pitiless because we will still have a huge price to pay to gain victory.

When I enlisted, things were different: it was a question of essential rescue and of sacrifice for an ideal. Now, the rescue is no longer necessary, and to be honest, I doubt that my ideals will be realised—not at any rate through military victory.

I applied for my present mission because I was embittered by having lost three years of my life and I wanted to play a personal part in ensuring that those responsible for all this chaos and suffering should pay the price. Is there any need for Gérard to do the same? No, and yet he probably will.

When I was seventeen, I formed the view that it should be possible for everyone to live happily. I sincerely believed it, as I was still a child, everything was still absurdly simple, and I had not heard the devil crying out in Faust, 'I see alone mankind's self-torturing pains.' I did not yet know how ridiculous it was to think life as beautiful and simple as it seemed to be. I chuckle when I re-read my old diaries and my essays.

And yet, if ever the world is to become a planet on which life is pleasant, it will be thanks to those who have managed to keep childish ideals alive in their hearts.

Basta! Thank God life in this camp does not leave us much time for dreams and morbid introspection. There is of course a lot of administration work, but also a lot of physical fitness training which is hard, but, as long as we have time for it, everyone enjoys it. I have just gained my wings, so I'm still feeling very pleased and proud.

Please give my love to your mother and to my uncle Felix, and I send my good wishes to you all for a happy new year.

Lionel.

1 January 1944
Lt Mosséri, "A" Battery RSR, Raiding Forces, MEF

Dearest Mother,

I've been working very hard for the last few weeks and time
has simply flown. So much so that when the New Year arrived
without warning I was taken by surprise, and only just gathered
my wits in time to make a wish that in this year we would at last
be reunited, and that the long and laborious preparations we
have all made might finally bear fruit.

Now I have a few days' rest, and I am feeling strangely
relaxed—it's a purely physical reaction, but it is having other
consequences too. I feel closer to you all than I have done for
a long time, since for the time being I have been less conscious
of an irritating aspect of my life, so have more leisure to think
of you.

Today is New Year's Day, and it has dawned to superb
weather. The room in the hotel where I have been spending
a couple of days of leave is flooded with sunlight and pure air.
I am on the top of Mount Carmel, and admiring the beautiful
bay. Everything around me is peaceful. My body is enjoying
several sensations it had almost forgotten: I have been able to
sleep as long as I needed to, and I am relishing the memory
of a hot bath when I got up, and the pleasant clean smell of
the disinfectant in the shiny white-tiled bathroom. I can still
taste my delicious breakfast and, delightfully, I have absolutely
nothing I need to do today, all day. For the next 24 hours, I
shall be neither too hot nor too cold, neither hungry nor thirsty;
in fact I am at peace with the world. So I have leisure to dream,

and I am dreaming of you. What are you doing this morning, you and your three men? No doubt you are all together—how I would love to be with you!

I remember one night when I was very small: you were looking beautiful, wearing an evening gown, looking like a fairy or a queen, I'm not sure which, but you were quite certainly my very own mother, standing by my bed and promising to come back soon; now it's my turn to make that promise. At Christmas, I suddenly had a fierce longing to leave the camp, steal an aeroplane, and fly over to join you. Why that day? I'm not quite sure. We weren't given any leave, but we had a very jolly Christmas. We played outrageous games – a game of rugby with fifty men on each side, and anything was allowed. To recover, we had a superb meal at which, according to long custom, the officers served their men at table.

After dinner, we had a visit from a well-known actress: young, pretty, desirable and yet so unreal! In a rather Proustian scenario, our general had 'forcibly' brought her here from Cairo to spend a few hours with us.

This pampered doll-like creature was suddenly wrenched from her natural habitat and plonked in the middle a large tent, surrounded by several dozen men. They are big lads, strong, of course, and built up even more by their training. As they watched her, they suddenly and violently realised that they hadn't even spoken to a woman for weeks. I was nervous that she would not realise this, but, bless her, something must have alerted her. As if by magic, she turned off her provocative behaviour and became maternal. As if to children, she gently sang old English ballads and romantic Christmas songs.

The others were all transported, and I was able to observe

them objectively, since for me these songs don't carry the same memories. Even the toughest faces softened. The girl chose just the right moment to revert from being an angel and become an attractive, desirable woman. I was not affected, and surprised myself by wondering what she must be feeling, standing on a table and being the focal point of desire for so many men, embodying so many dreams and wishes. She left, finally. I wonder if she is enough of an artist to have enjoyed the experience, for it would be a shame if it were wasted.

It was then that I suddenly wanted to filch a plane.

The telephone has just rung. A friend is asking if I want to go for a game of squash. I've re-read this letter, in which I had hoped to say so much, but is so vague and says so little. Shall I carry on? No, I shan't. However, I do promise to write you a less fanciful letter very soon, one that is more down to earth and won't attempt to convey the somewhat inchoate feelings that I had wanted to share with you.

All my very best wishes for your birthday and for the New Year.

With much love from

Lionel.

(Original in English)
L. Mosséri, Lt,
Advanced HQ, R&S c/o Advanced HQ Force 133,CMF
14 March, 1944

Dearest Mother,

Suddenly, I find myself almost completely becalmed, with
scarcely anything to do beyond the daily routine.

It's a pleasant change after the long and arduous training
we've had, I can assure you, especially as we are in comfortable
accommodation in a little rural village in Italy. My comrades
and my men, though, are jittery. They are fed up with the lack
of action—we have been hoping for a long time that by now we
would be up to our eyes in it.

For the last few days, I have been trying to escape from
a very vigilant, aggressive and unattractive 'mama', a very
pretty young Italian girl, and to find a passable nurse among
the nearby hospital personnel. Both these attempts have failed
miserably, so I have given up. I have now withdrawn into my
ivory tower and draped myself in complete indifference. From
the height of my superiority I am watching the even more
pathetic failures of my comrades, who are further handicapped
by having no knowledge of Italian.

I am having more luck elsewhere. I have found an excellent
local library that the Germans did not have time to loot, where
I have spent many happy hours. Yesterday, when I was tiring
of the somewhat easy, and always pompous and grandiloquent
style of Gabriele d'Annunzio, I found with great delight a
translation of Lettres de mon moulin.[71] Apart from Sapho,
which I read about eight months ago, I had not read any

Daudet for years. The realistic style and the moving simplicity of the stories were like a breath of fresh air in a musty room. His characters are human, lively, and lack the unhealthy subtlety of Saroyan or the rather scornful intellectualism of Huxley; the hypersensitivity of Auden or Maugham. I bathed in joy, rather as I was when I discovered the fairy tales of Andersen, all those years ago—do you remember?

As well as reading, I am doing some military training. I went with my men on manoeuvres the other day. I gave my sergeant—I sent you a picture of him recently, along with one of me and one of my corporal—our two machine-guns, and entered a house about four thousand metres away. His orders were to shoot at the house so I could gauge the effect of our weapons at that distance. Two minutes before the appointed time, and in spite of the notices I had posted to warn that the area would be used for military exercises, I happened to notice an old peasant peacefully starting to work his field. I shouted at him to get out, but he didn't move. So I rushed towards him. Improbable as it may seem, the stupid old boy answered back. I was furious, and told him that if he refused to move he would certainly be killed, then I turned back and ran towards the house.

I had just got behind a little embankment when the bullets started flying. My sergeant had adjusted his aim properly, but the bullets were landing to one side because of the wind. I was about eighty metres from the house and on the edge of the target area. It was most unpleasant to be caught out in the open like that. We had agreed that there would be a seven-second pause when he stopped firing, so that the sergeant could adjust his aim. I worked out that with a bit of luck I would be able to

[71] A collection of short stories by Alphonse Daudet.

get to the house before he started firing again. As soon as the firing stopped, I hurtled towards the house. My calculations were just about right, for I had to dive into a little furrow in the ground about fifteen metres from the house when he started spraying bullets again. This time I was really scared.

As a machine-gun operator, I was only too well aware of the danger I was in, especially as my sergeant was unfortunately rather a good shot. He had assessed the wind and made the necessary corrections, and this time I was in the middle of the storm. The little dip I was in, and a huge dose of luck, saved me. While he was shooting, I was afraid, and furious. Furious because I was thinking how stupid it would be to die simply because an old fool refused to follow orders and also because I felt there was an odd kind of disloyalty in my sergeant having the advantage over me: in a real battle, there would be smoke and some shots coming at him, so he would be prevented from aiming so carefully.

I reached the house at last. We had agreed that the shooting exercise would stop for twenty minutes, during which I went to see how my old peasant was doing. He was on the ground, and had not been in any danger at any point. I gave him the telling-off of his life.

Two civilians then went along the road past the house. At that moment I hated the whole Italian nation most cordially, so I ordered them to stop and, as they did not obey, I pulled out my revolver and fired on one of their wheels. I then had the second scare of my rather-too-lively morning, as the other cyclist fell to the ground. I thought I had misfired and wounded him. He was unhurt, and I got rid of them by promising them both that they would go to prison for disobeying military orders.

When I went back to my sergeant he asked why I was looking so flustered!

I have just received your two airmail letters of 28 January and 1 February. You must have started to write to my new address, so I hope that from now on your letters will reach me more quickly.

I have been feeling guilty about some of my long silences. It would be too easy to say—although it is true—that most of the time I am very busy, but unfortunately it's not quite as simple as that.

You see, dearest Mother, the truth is that this military life is so very different from the life for which my education prepared me, that even now, after three years of war, I'm not yet used to it. I have of course learned how to give orders, and have developed great physical endurance—these are the basic tools of my trade—but it's still not my life, somehow.

Emotionally and intellectually, I am still the same person I was when I last saw you. I have not become used to how boring routine and administrative tasks can be, to daily life and to the mediocrity of those with whom I share it. I live somewhat in the past, quite a lot in the future, and therefore very little in the present.

The times when I feel I am really alive are very few, and yet these are the only ones I want to share with you. I wonder how long I can carry on like this?

Today it is three years to the day since I first set foot in a military barracks and put on my first uniform. There have been times of great enthusiasm since, and times of disappointment and boredom. On other days, I have been cold, hungry, dead tired and violently homesick for home and for you. But, apart from a few times, I don't feel I've been living all this time—it hasn't really been part of my life.

I know you will understand me… but just now, please don't feel sorry for me. You would be taking pity on a patient who had undergone an operation for an ailment with which he could have lived, if he had been given an anaesthetic. I would love to hear you say, 'You will soon, very soon, be back with me; I will teach you to live again, and to take life up again, starting from the moment when we were separated.'

Goodbye, Mother dearest, and once again may God bless you for all that you have done and for all that you stand for.

Lionel.

April, 1944

256094 L. Mosséri, Lt.

A. Bty, Advanced HQ, Force 133, CMF

Dearest Mother,

At last I have the opportunity to write a lengthier letter and to give you a few details of my life, which has really been extremely full for the last few weeks.

First, you must by now have a general idea of the operations I am engaged in, but unfortunately I'm not allowed to give you any details. I've always been open with you, dearest Mother, and this is certainly not the moment I would chose to change that. So please believe me when I tell you that I think my present occupation is less dangerous than an infantryman's.

The work is harder, the training is more intense and life in general is more difficult, but so very much more interesting!

So please don't worry. Just remember what I promised when I became an officer—I will keep that promise and that is all that matters. There may be times when I am not able to contact you, but if you don't hear from me for a while, you should receive a military telegram every month to tell you how I am.

I am now in Italy. There are traces here and there of Allied bombings, but not many, since the only targets were those of military significance, and those have been wiped out. The towns and villages are not like London, for example, where the Germans have simply dropped bombs randomly.

The Italian population is divided into two very clear groups: the rich and the poor. The rich live well and seem very little affected by the war, which must give them great satisfaction, since they appear to be entirely devoid of any sense of civic obligation. The poor live in terrible conditions in dreadful hovels and medieval conditions.

This is not due, however, to the war. There is plenty of evidence that the situation is due to an autarkic economy and a history of poverty that the fascist regime has not even attempted to overcome during its twenty-five years of rule. There is no spirit among the population, no sense of pride or dignity.

Italian officers walk the streets unshaven and poorly dressed. If they are the leaders, it is hardly surprising that the watchword among the population is, 'It's over, basta.' Not that this is very fair, since these same characters would be only too pleased to parade themselves as worthy representatives of a new order. It's too easy to wage war when it simply involves gunning down savages and attacking a nation already defeated, or advancing a few kilometres in the desert on a few frontier posts with an army of 200,000 men and then, when things go badly, to say, 'Oh well, it would have been nice to win. So long as we thought we might, we behaved like pigs, but since we weren't allowed to have our own way, let's stop playing the game.' Either these people still firmly hold to their fascist ideals, in which case they should still think of us as enemies— and they certainly don't seem to—or they should have fought tooth and nail against the dictatorship, and they didn't do that either. They have however—with a few notable exceptions— displayed a complete lack of civic courage, and therefore deserve only scorn.

For the first time since I enlisted—with the possible exception of those four months I spent guarding an airfield as a private—I feel directly responsible for a small part of the war. If something is not clear, it is not French, and so I'll have another go: for the first time, I am a danger to the Germans, not an inert potential danger, but a real danger. I matter. What I do and what I think can make a difference. I am no longer a rifleman learning to be a soldier; a cadet hoping to become an officer; a lieutenant learning his trade. At last, I am an instrument helping to destroy that monstrous edifice: Hitler. At last, I am truly able to wage war and, because I am involved, I find it more interesting than ever before. This is why I find no joy in meeting even slightly friendly Italians. It simply proves that there is an almost complete lack of any true democracy in this country, or of an honest and perceptive electorate. What is the good of war if no phoenix can arise from the ashes? It was not serious to lose young German officers in 1940, for there would be many others to take their place; to maintain the same ideals and the same dreams.

Even without thinking of death, it seems hard to be particularly optimistic about the future. The English are an odd people. They seem able to encompass paradoxes more extreme than the most fanciful of Frenchmen, and that is why I am fearful. I fear that the magnificent energy of Dunkirk has now dried up, and that boredom and indifference will set in as soon as war ends.

After Germany is defeated, the United Nations may have an opportunity unique in the history of mankind to institute an everlasting peace. But if we do not manage to eradicate the real causes of war, then we shall inevitably be on the road to self-destruction.

For the first time, a civilisation has given its creators the means to make ever further progress, as well as the means to destroy themselves completely. Both Greek civilisation, which scorned material work, and Hindu civilisation, with its caste system, puts limits on their action and undermines their very raison d'être.

For the first time, it will be possible to set up a democratic government as Rousseau intended it. We shall be able to abolish the class system through the levelling effect of education. We shall be able to meet the economic needs of people and even guarantee them some leisure time. We should also all, for the first time, be free of our old preconceptions. And finally, for the first time, most of the world's population ardently wishes for peace, simultaneously.

So why am I so fearful when there seems to be such a fair hope of success?

I fear, because the world at large, having understood the need to destroy Nazism, seems to have forgotten that although this is a necessary condition for peace and progress, it is not of itself sufficient.

Roosevelt and Churchill firmly believe, no doubt, in the principles of the Atlantic Charter, but their implementation depends above all on the cooperation of all of society. I honestly don't believe that a single Englishman will be prepared to exchange his rights and privileges as an Englishman for those he might enjoy, but which may for a while be less profitable to him, as a citizen of the world. As a general rule, and without quite knowing why, the average Englishman baulks at the thought of sharing citizenship with the United States. So he understands even less that it is not possible for one person to enjoy certain liberties and rights while the rest of the community is denied them, and that the freedom of a single man is at least as important as his own.

The British soldier dreams of getting home to his family, of going out with his fiancée on a Saturday evening, of holding her hand in a luxurious cinema after a good meal. These dreams may seem harmless, and less likely to start a war than the dreams of German soldiers. But in fact they are just as dangerous, because they acknowledge that some evils will continue, and there is no desire to root them out. Freedom is not an abstract, static notion, but an ever-changing reality, and its shifting contours must continually be identified.

My religious beliefs have hardly changed since I last saw you, and I still firmly believe in whatever gods there may be. Now, however, all the misery I see befalling apparently innocent mankind around me would long ago have destroyed all faith within me, if I did not honestly believe that most of those suffering do so because of their inertia during peace-time, and for their failure to build a just world when they had the opportunity.

I have promised myself that I will take an active part, after the war, in the construction of peace. I shall write in newspapers, speak on radio or in the streets if need be, to prevent history repeating itself at even greater cost. If everyone had done that between 1920 and 1938 it seems impossible to believe such a collective civilising effort would not have been able to overcome Germany and prevent the current massacre.

I've re-read what I have written. I realise that my French has really suffered, and my style leaves much to be desired. If parrain is worried, please reassure him. I shall only need to spend a few days under his influence and he will no longer need to be ashamed of me. I am, however, now very proud of my writing in English, especially when writing to D. Have you received our photos? She complains bitterly that of all officers she has happened upon, I am the one who is the worst correspondent. But I really have very little time.

I miss her badly here, and it's no use denying that I really love her very much. Unfortunately I have chosen the time and place very badly. I do hope that when I see her again I won't have changed too much and we shall still get on well. I received your telegram about Gérard. I am delighted to hear he is in the French naval air force and I very much look forward to hearing from him. I also look forward to hearing from you, as I have not received any letters for some time, no doubt because they are pursuing me from one address to another.

Please give parrain my fondest love, and I send it to you too, and a long, everlasting kiss.

Lionel.

L Mosséri, Lt.
4 Section A Bty, c/o Advanced HW RSR , Force 266 CMF
2 May, 1944

Dearest Mother,

At this very moment I am certainly more depressed and miserable than I have been at any point since leaving America. Maybe it is too easy to pick up pen and paper just now and to pour out my sorrow to you, but really, Mother, I feel so small, so alone and so helpless, and you will understand...

A few weeks ago, we came back from a field operation and, after a few days' rest, my two best friends and the captain under whom we served went off again. I had to stay behind as neither my men nor I were needed, and I was left under the command of a man I don't like.

A few days later, we quarrelled, and for the first time in three years' service, I have to admit that I was insubordinate. Of course, I was disciplined, and if I had not had a good service record the colonel might well have been much harder on me. I had absolutely no desire to stay in my current unit, since my friends and my commanding officer had left, so I applied for a transfer to a different unit. A brief interview showed I was just the kind of officer they needed, and not only did I have all the right qualifications to do the work, but also there were not many others with similar capabilities.

I was very pleased, and went to see my colonel, who coldly refused to release me because, he said, I was indispensable to him too.

This may not all seem very important, but there are other things too. Also, it seems forever since I last received a letter either from you or from D. The post is not working, and so for the first time I have had enough. I am fed up and furious, grumpy and careless of whatever may happen to me. My only hope is that they may find an officer to take my place in my present unit, but unfortunately that seems unlikely.

I am just back from three days leave, which I spent, doing nothing. I was on strike against the whole world in my hotel room. My only pleasure was to take up to three baths per day and to read not Homer's Iliad, but a book on the theory of Greek history.

I have just re-read this letter. I think I had better stop. I'm off into the mountains for a few days tomorrow, alone with my men. I shall feel better by the time I get back and I shall no doubt regret writing this letter. Never mind.

Lots and lots of love from

Lionel.

Letter to his brother

End of May 1944

A Bty, Advanced HQ RSR

c/o Advanced HQ Force 133, CMF

My dear Gérard,

It's now four years since we last saw each other in America. During that time you have continued to live a more or less normal life. You are no longer a boy, but a man, having come through various natural changes.

As a student, you must have dreamed the same dreams, read the same ideas, developed the same passion for certain ideals, enjoyed the same feelings as I did, and as all others have done who have had the good fortune to receive the kind of education we have received. As you made this long transition, there was very little I could say to you, as my life has been so very different. You would not have understood, hence my scarce correspondence.

About a month ago I heard from Mother that you were about to enlist, and I was about to write to you when I suddenly received orders to leave, and found myself with practically no warning involved in action. I am writing to you now, using a munitions box for a table, somewhere in...[72] in a theatre of war where we have recently achieved a fairly significant victory. Just now, nothing is happening, so as you see I am making the most of it.

In a few weeks, it will be your turn to enter the armed forces, and I wish you good luck and good hunting. It is of course possible and probable that the war may end before you have had a chance to see any action. I calculate (and I hope I am right) that it will take about nine months for you to qualify as an officer pilot, and much may happen between now and then. The forces massed against Germany are huge, overwhelming. But just as we in England resisted in 1940, the Germans may try to do the same, and we can only hope that they will not succeed. Anyway, whatever happens, you have now left the protection of the family and its way of life in order to make your own way in a world that is less pleasant and yet more real, less hospitable and yet more fertile—a world very different from what you have known so far.

[72] Yugoslavia.

I would love to be able to tell you life is wonderful, smiling, and jolly; that the people you will meet are modern knights; and that you will find yourself surrounded by courage, honesty and progress. Such thoughts are fine as an ideal and as rose-tinted as a dream, but they are only a dream. It may be disagreeable at times, but whatever happens you will have to live life as it presents itself, not as you dream it to be.

So please don't be too disappointed at what you find. For a start, you will notice that you have so far in life enjoyed a level of comfort that most of your comrades have not even dreamed of.

You will probably be more at ease as an airman than I have been in the army, but don't expect to spend your time in fine airfields such as one might see in the cinema.

You will no doubt be stuffed into a hangar with dozens of strangers, sleeping on the ground, doing chores, and only after a few weeks will you begin to feel like a soldier and have learned to stay clean in an environment that isn't clean.

All this is not really very important—you will learn quickly and get used to it all. The difficult part will be getting on with the others. For a start, you will almost certainly, meet people of a kind you didn't even know existed, funny blokes whose language and ideas will seem completely foreign.

Don't say too much at first, for they won't understand you and will instinctively be jealous and hostile. You'll build a relationship bit by bit, and you will have much to learn from them, for they are worthy people who have had a hard life in a harsh reality.

This is all rather difficult to explain. I would advise you not to lose heart, as things have a way of sorting themselves out.

Time is less precious than you may have thought. Say little, be friendly and obliging. Obey orders without question, and look after your health carefully.

This last point is very important. My men, and therefore I too, have the reputation of being among the best trained and toughest in the army. They don't drink, and sleep a lot. They do as much sport as possible, though without it becoming an obsession.

Smoke as little as possible. If you feel the need, go out with women, but take all the necessary precautions against venereal disease. If you should happen to contract something, go straight to the doctor. However, I should warn you that occasional relationships with women will not relieve emotional tension. Be careful not to confuse the two.

I would have liked to send you a carefully composed letter, but as you know, my circumstances are unfortunately far from ideal. For the moment, I am fairly comfortable, but only relatively so.

Write as soon as you can, old boy, a good long letter. I promise I will write back and I'm sure I will be able to help sometimes. You are a man now, doing a man's work. Once again, good luck and good hunting!

Lionel.

PART 5

Idyll

L IONEL WAS KEEN to be a fully committed soldier, and
had therefore always sought to keep himself free of
romantic attachments. He had a fond and completely platonic
relationship with his great friend V., but otherwise there were
no women in his life.

In the summer of 1943 he met, for the first time, a young
woman with whom he could contemplate sharing his life. He
met Miss D. in Cairo, and told his mother that he had become
very fond of her. There was an initial "coup de foudre" period
of infatuation, followed by a quarrel and then a reconciliation.
Lionel then volunteered for the specialist Raiding Support
Regiment and left for Palestine. He wrote to Miss D. very
infrequently, but his letters, which are in English, are
remarkable, and must be read from beginning to end. One
of them is confessional, in the sense of a thorough self-
examination displaying neither false pride nor false humility.
The two young people never made a formal commitment to
each other. The idyll was fruitless.

5 Coy No. 2 J.T.D.
KRRC

26 August, 1943

Dearest Mother,

I had six really fabulous days in Cairo. Much tennis and swimming. The first evening, Helen took me to a reception at the Belgian consulate. It was a lovely evening, with many charming young ladies, particularly one called D. She has been in Cairo for six months and is working in one of the ministries.

She is the first girl since Colette with whom I have been able to talk rather than dance, and go for walks with rather than to the theatre, or the cinema. She is both intelligent and cultured, and is the prettiest thing I ever saw: dark, fine hair, beautiful blue eyes, gentle but sparkling, very white teeth, slender and graceful.

We spent six perfect days, as she was also on leave. But we are at war, and this is the twentieth century. I had to return to camp, and she to her office. We were only too aware that we could do nothing but wait. I am a soldier, so there are risks I cannot take, and she does not want me to feel responsible for her, or that in the period immediately after the war she should be a burden. So we are being modern and logical, following heads rather than hearts, living as we do in the age of the machine, in a brave new world.

I will send you a photo of her. I would love you to meet her as soon as possible, and I am sure you will like her a lot.

With lots of love from
Lionel.

5 Coy—3 Bn KRRC
BMEF

20 October 1943

Dearest Mother,

Last week, I received a pack of letters from you which finally reached me from England. The most recent is admittedly dated 10 May, but after such a long silence this hardly matters and I read and re-read every letter with the greatest possible pleasure.

It was a Sunday, and I had been to the bank in Sophie's little car. I was with D., but she was unable to claim my attention for the next three-quarters of an hour. She behaved very well, given the provocation. Instead of assiduously courting her, the young man for whose benefit she was wearing a new dress and a new hairstyle was ignoring her, when usually her beautiful eyes could wordlessly impose her will and command obedience.

However, I have been given a solemn warning. You are the only person, dearest Mother, who is allowed thus to distract my attention, or to have any influence on either my ideas, or my dreams.

I went back to camp that very evening, happier than I had been since leaving America, and the happiness continued, as the following week was really very pleasant.

I love you all very, very much.

Lionel.

Letter to Miss D. (written in English)
L. Mosséri, Lt., RSR, Raiding Forces HQ, MEF
25 November, 1943

My darling,

I am writing to you from somewhere in Palestine. Our camp is enclosed between a range of small mountains and the sea. After so many months in the desert, the sparse vegetation and the wind off the sea, which is reinvigorating and stimulating, and yet strangely calming and peaceful, inordinately delight me.

My days have been full of thoughts of you recently. Immediately after that afternoon in Cairo I was overcome by a great fury towards you and deep self-pity.

That evening, a young woman I had met at my aunt's must have wondered how a young man could be so rude, especially as I think—I'm not certain—she was rather nice. I went back to camp the next day determined to take refuge in my tent.

But there, next to my bed as always, your picture was smiling at me—a bit sadly, perhaps—and suddenly said to me very gently and calmly, 'Don't take on so, my darling, I beg of you. Just remember the good times we have had together.' And, by some miracle, that is what I did.

I remembered laughing in the swimming pool on our first evening at the Pyramids, and I remembered the party we gave. As long as I live I shall remember how enchanting you looked with that pink rose in your hair and the Spanish-looking shawl. You were the embodiment of a thousand dreams, a shadow haunting my imagination and miraculously given flesh— Galatea brought to life. You were the unwritten symphony, its notes suddenly bursting forth like an impetuous stream breaching a dam and escaping.

And as the evening melted into night, any bitterness I had felt also seeped away, and like the Ancient Mariner I felt full of regret and of fear, 'For all averred I killed the bird... ', and other lines shot through my mind in a flash:

Yet each man kills the thing he loves...
Some love too little, some too long,
Some sell and others buy.
Some do the deed with many tears,
And some without a sigh;
For each man kills the thing he loves,
Yet each man does not die.

My darling, please don't ever believe I was not fully aware of what an inestimable treasure you are. My crime was that, while knowing it full well, I was unable to be fair to you. I was clumsily holding a fragile thing, while staying silent, dumb, and yet brutally damaging it.

My one hope is that one day in the future, loving you still as I do now, I may have the opportunity to express myself more clearly, to find a wavelength that suits us both so we can communicate with no outside interference.

It is unfortunate that we have met at this stage of my life. The army has neither stimulated nor developed me. Rather, it has tended to make me withdraw into myself. Spending a month at the depot had in any case depressed me even further.

In many ways, the life I am leading here is one I have long sought. Mostly, the men are splendid, and the officers do not have the affected superficiality of my previous unit. Socially, they are of a slightly lower class, so their good manners are more genuine. Some have seen quite a bit of service in Spain, Finland and China—so they are chaps with ideals! Our job as parachutists gives us more scope for individual initiative, and what we will be doing will be truly worthwhile.

In a few days, I shall be starting parachute jumps, and I should soon gain my wings. It all helps. It also helps that I am physically exhausted at the end of each day. Even though my days are so full, however, I can never shut you out.

You have come into my life, my darling, and you are there forever. You appear at the most bizarre moments, in the most unexpected places, wearing clothes I have never seen you wear, saying things I have never heard you say. And yet it really is you.

When we meet again, even if it is soon, I shall have changed much. But I know that whatever happens we shall recognise each other despite all the changes.

I will write soon, my darling. Be happy, I beg of you, and please, you too, remember.

Lionel.

Letter to Miss D. (written in English)

Early 1944

My darling,

Writing this letter is one of the most difficult things I have ever had to do and—even if I finish it and it is absolutely honest, as I firmly intend right now—the bravest of my life. There are several different kinds of courage, darling, but for me there is only one that matters, that I respect, and it's what a father wishes for his son: the courage to be honest towards himself. It is hard for a young man to lay his soul bare before the one he loves, because there is no glory in such an act. You might even think it cowardly, in the last analysis, to cheat you of any illusions about me, but I'm feeling too confused to enter into discussing that.

I should have written this letter long ago. That I have not can be attributed partly to a lack of courage and partly to my optimistic nature.

You know—this at least I have told you—what a reviving effect you have had on me. I don't quite know how I have spent the last two years. I have lived in part by remembering the past, in part by dreaming of the future, and in part in a fantasy world of my own imagination. Now, though, I have met you, and I no longer have either the right or the wish to continue this kind of existence. Hence the need for this disagreeable task.

Now I have started writing, however, I am simply temporising and delaying. So let's be done with this long preamble and begin at the beginning, as I should have done from the start.

For most of my life, with the notable exception of the year I spent at the Sorbonne, I had the misfortune of being unpopular in my immediate circle, and sometimes even—and this is far worse—of being an object of ridicule. And yet I always felt that I was better than most of those around me. If I am right, then none of that matters. But am I right?

At school, at least until I was fifteen, I did not display any particular intelligence. I know only one thing: I was always trying to reach an objective that was a little beyond my grasp. I did reasonably well in my exams, however. This surprised most of my teachers, apart from the only two whose opinion mattered to me: the headmaster at Gresham's, who always had, and still has, confidence in me and who has had a considerable influence on my character, and my history teacher, who had enormous bearing on my way of thinking and of working.

So by the time I left Gresham's I had done nothing remarkable other than acquiring a degree of unpopularity that is difficult to account for, given that I was a boy who—and I can say this in all honesty—was always straight and loyal, did not tell on others and had never in any way broken any of the important rules of life.

I was quite good at sport; I had proved my worth in the clubs and societies that I had joined, and I had made one good friend.

I was very sensitive. I had a profound desire to widen my intellectual horizons—are such things enough to justify the feeling of being superior to others? I was not after all an artist; I had not created anything except for one bad play.

At the end of the Easter term, I left Gresham's to go to France and prepare to take my baccalauréat in two months by taking private lessons in Paris. Compared to the exams one takes at the same age in Anglo-Saxon countries, the baccalauréat is very testing, so I had to work hard, especially as I had not had the same intellectual preparation as others who had spent their lives studying a curriculum attuned to this final exam. My languages helped a lot; I knew enough in physics, history and mathematics, and under the guidance of an amazing little man—a kind of magician[73]—I learned for the first time how to write an essay, to put my ideas together and to understand the ideal of beauty that I had glimpsed on my own. I gradually realised the magic power

[73] Mr Norman.

that words have, and slowly and painfully started to put my feelings down on paper—and I passed the exam. There again, though, this was nothing unusual, and I am sure hundreds of French students must have passed the exam as well or better than I that same year.

During the holidays of that summer, I read up on philosophy, rested and sampled the magical delights of the Norwegian islands. I was starting to spread my wings. At home I was living, for the first time, with my mother and my stepfather. For the first time I was able to watch a great man living and working, and to observe his method of thinking. For the first time, I learned how to make the most of my time off by organising it, going to the best concerts and plays. Almost as soon as I had left the little island[74] and arrived in England on my way to Oxford, war was declared. Not long after, my parents asked me to return to Paris for reasons that were nothing to do with my education, but which were to prepare me to become an officer in the French army in due course.

The year I spent in Paris was the only time in my life I remember being completely and continuously happy. Before, there had of course been happy moments, for instance when skiing in Switzerland and in the Savoie, or riding, or summers spent at Deauville swimming in the sea and playing tennis, and there had been a little moment of paradise on earth on the Norwegian island half-way between the blue of the sea and the blue of the sky, where I found peace, strength and happiness – a carefree and healthy happiness.

Even then, however, I was trying, straining, to attain something that was just out of reach, I was always anxious, forever seeking, often friendless.

---

[74] The Ile de la Cité, an island in the Seine in the heart of Paris.

During that first winter of the war I discovered a new language—that of the law—a new vocabulary and new horizons stretching out of sight. With more force than ever before I was struck by the power of the written word, of the law, which is composed in the quiet atmosphere of a study, but can change the destiny of men, and build a new and ordered society. I developed a passion for research in economics, which is the determining force in nearly all human activity. I shall never forget my feelings on first reading the introduction to Marshall's Principles.

For the first time in my life, I was completely happy. I worked well and methodically. I also enjoyed more than ever before living in a family, something I had not known until then. My stepfather was having an increasing influence on the way I thought.

I saw quite a bit of men such as Robbins, Beveridge, Lippmann, Rueff and Siegfried. I can say I was brought up in the French liberal tradition of Rousseau, Voltaire and Sieyès and the Declaration of the Rights of Man. I was impatient for the day when I would be able to fight alongside other men who thought as I did.

I also had some good times of relaxation at Saint Cloud on Sundays, and at the Théâtre Français on Saturdays, where I saw Vera Korène playing. I also met Colette, whom I have mentioned to you.

Then all this came to an end. I saw France collapse. I was in Bordeaux, and saw the panic and complete lack of dignity. I spoke there with Bernstein, Reynaud, Jules Romains and many others. I saw a great nation fall apart with my own eyes... All I had admired and valued was crumbling under the weight of Hitler's power. If I had been able to succeed in the France of 1940—and I'm sure I would have succeeded—can I hope, without fooling myself, to succeed in the brave new world of 1946, with its lowest common denominator and the superficiality of its culture and civilisation, and the tendency towards—and this may seem paradoxical—regimentation and the denial of most classical ideals?

There were great discoveries in America too—Hutchins at the University of Chicago, Lippmann, Kohler at Wisconsin: the miracle of modern industry as the solution to social problems. Meanwhile, France—the mother-country of the civil code—was enacting racial laws... I have since become poignantly aware of the massive force of inertia through which most of the American population oppose real progress.

I enlisted in England and failed to progress for nearly two years. I was an average officer, liked by a few and misunderstood by others, speaking a completely different language from most of my fellow officers, who smiled when they listened to me.

Was I right? Were they wrong? This evening I saw a film. It had all the necessary ingredients for a tragi-comedy: pathos, contradictory human emotions, a clear analysis of love, of jealousy, of neurosis, and it even had good dancing. As a whole, it was an intelligent satire on modern society. As I came out I said, 'Excellent!' The officer I was with said, 'Execrable!'

If I have to live after the war in the same company as I keep now, I very much doubt that I shall do well, and I shall not manage to get back to the France of 1940.

It is better that you should have a clear knowledge of the person with whom you would be called to live your life—a revolutionary—for I do not share my ideals with those around me any more than I share my joys and my values. If, after all this, you still want me, my darling, then you must know that I need you more than life itself. To me, you represent mercy, simplicity, adventure and discovery, gentleness, love and understanding.

Thank you for reading all this jumble of feelings so long withheld. Please try to make sense of them. I've been no help to you, I know, but you have already helped me so much.

Forever yours,

Lionel.

Letter to Miss D. (written in English)
Captain Mosséri, ISSU 6, BNAF
26 July, 1944

My darling,

I received two of your letters last week, one from May and one from June. I was both soothed and stimulated as I read them. This is no paradox, as you have given me a glimpse of happiness and you have made me yearn to achieve it. It seems to me, darling, that you have changed a lot in this last year. Who knows—when we meet again I may find my little girl changed into a young woman. And I know I shall be delighted. It is always difficult to talk to children unless one is oneself either very young or very old.

Whatever happens, though, please don't let yourself be overcome by pessimism and bitterness. I can well imagine that life in Cairo could easily lead one to such a frame of mind. Please avoid it at all costs. The defeat of Hitler is a necessary condition to winning the war, but it is not sufficient. We must be ready to create something new and different not only from his New Order, but also from the old order in which we lived before the war—an order which gave rise to Nazism and its monstrous beliefs.

We shall only succeed if we are optimistic and trust others. This doesn't mean one should be so idealistic that one is not able to face brutal facts. On the contrary, we have to see things as they really are. I know only too well there are many selfish little men in the world—men who are mean even in their vices. But, my darling, there are also the others—millions of others, some of whom have always had ideals; others now have had this ideal shown to them: 'The torn veil will reveal to you... '

Europe today is nothing but a mass of tortured and chaotic humanity, but the suffering has already inspired great actions, and it will inspire many more.

The whole world will soon hear of the acts of selflessness, of sheer courage and of superhuman heroism during these four dreadful years—deeds done by unknown, simple people, tradesmen, rural teachers, drivers, labourers—in short, by people who have shown themselves in their true light during these terrible years and have demonstrated qualities which would not otherwise have been revealed under our old system.

This, my darling, is why you must not develop a twisted view of the world simply because you happen to have been surrounded for the moment by those who are the dregs of society.

You must make every effort to meet those outside your immediate circle who are interesting, full of energy and ideas... not simply those who are amusing live wires. Try to get to know artists, writers, academics and scientists... rather like that couple from Palestine of whom you wrote. They are the only ones that matter—they will build the world of the future.

You see, my darling, whatever name you give them and subtle definitions you apply, there are only two ways of seeing the world:

One can either say, 'Man is evil, vile, selfish and a traitor; he cannot be allowed to be free, for he will abuse freedom; this is why his every movement must be controlled, directed, and his every act decided for him.' Or you can say that on the whole man is good; that he is evil only due to abnormal circumstances, but at the deepest level he is worthy of his freedom. Man should therefore be free. His actions should be decided for him only to the extent necessary to prevent a few individuals from imposing their interests and will on the majority, and to create conditions that will enable his natural goodness to emerge.

This philosophy can at first seem simplistic, but it is far from so. In the end, any political or economic doctrine is based either on optimism and trust, or on pessimism and distrust. Myself, I prefer trust. I am so pleased you received my news. Your photograph has always come everywhere with me and I hope with all my heart that we shall meet again soon.

At the moment, I am temporarily attached to a French parachute and commando regiment. The officers and the men are all from the elite. In order to join the battalion, the men have to have escaped from France, and the officers are career officers of the best sort. I am enjoying it so much that I might ask to be transferred to the French army in order to fight with them.

Maybe you remember in one of my letters that I tried to explain the team spirit in which, with my men, I would like to fight the good fight. Well, I have finally found those men and that spirit; I am happy—happier than I have been for a long time.

Goodbye, my darling, with all my love. And please remember that 'later, in a better world, I shall require greater love and fuller knowledge of you.'

Lionel.

PS: 'I remember a coral branch, a flower of the transparent sea.'

PART 6

The French Campaign

L IONEL'S CORRESPONDENCE tells us very little about his service record in France. All his last letters were lost, except for one in which he tells his mother of his decision to transfer to the French army.

15 October, 1944

Dearest Mother,

I have not had any news from you for a long time, and I doubt you are receiving mine, for several reasons. So I am sending this letter via the American post. I will repeat a quick summary of my life during the past few weeks, in case you haven't received my earlier letters.

After I left my Raiding Forces regiment in Italy, I was attached to a unit doing the same kind of work – not in the Balkans but in France. At the last minute I wasn't able to go, so that I found myself without any specific employment in the week before D-Day. My commanding officer offered to loan me to the French commandos, while still keeping me on his books.

I so enjoyed serving with the commandos that I asked to be transferred to the French army. There was one important issue: as I had not previously served in the French army, I should in theory have been taken on as an infantryman. However, taking my eleven jumps into account, together with all the training I had done, Diethelm admitted me as an officer, but only as second lieutenant, which of course is not in the least important.

In this battalion, I have met Major Vallon, whose wife Suzanne knows you well. I met her when she was on leave from Italy, where she is doing splendid work as a doctor in the B army. Since then, to her husband's great disappointment, she has returned to France before him.

Our colonel is called Gambiez. He was in charge of operations in Corsica—the commando raids on the Italian coast and on Elba. He's one of the most remarkable men and one of the best soldiers I have ever met.

All our men and officers have escaped from France or from Germany. So this is really an elite unit in terms of training, moral and state of mind.

Unfortunately we still have to live with old administration and procurement systems, though the colonel tries to improve things. I very much hope that after the war men such as Gambiez will be given positions of trust and will be able to create a new, rejuvenated army full of enthusiasm and especially imbued with professional pride.

Even as it is now, the army of De Lattre de Tassigny is already magnificent, and I really hope that we shall soon be in the heart of Germany, ahead of the other Allied forces.

As soon as I arrived in France, I wrote to Paule, Renée and Guy, but I don't know whether they received my letters. I don't think I shall be able to get to Paris for the next few months. In case it is of use to them, I have given them my postal address and I hope I shall receive news of them.

As for news of you, my poor Mother, I have now given up on all the letters you may have written since June. They would have to go through such a succession of military addresses, from the British army to the French army, and through so many different military zones, that I think I shall only receive them after being demobilised. I am nevertheless looking forward to those that will reach me at the headquarters of the French First Army, postal sector 70930.

Until now, dearest Mother, I have kept my promise and nothing has happened to me: we have reached the last hundred metres. I shall finish the race unhurt and I really hope that at the start of next year we shall all be reunited.

With all my love,

Lionel.

Since we have no precise details from Lionel himself, I sought information from his commanding officers, his fellow officers and his men about what he did and the part he played in the military operation of the French Campaign. I am particularly grateful to Lieutenant-Colonel Vallon and Captain Ruais who were most helpful to my research.

The reader will recall that in June or July 1944, Lionel had been sent as an instructor to the English training facility at Staoueli, near Algiers, where parachutists trained to be dropped into France.

At the same time, French command decided to create a similar training facility at nearby Sidi-Ferruch, which would take only volunteers who had escaped France via the Pyrenees and Spain, and who were all very keen to engage in daring and dangerous missions.

The initial plan was for these units to be dropped by parachute behind German lines, in order to help the maquis in their work, especially in the Vercors and Limousin areas. Later, because of a shortage of aircraft, it was decided that the units would become commando units, trained to carry out surprise attacks on land. Each unit was made up of three sections, each of 130 men, and one section, hand-picked, for headquarters protection. The first unit of French commandos, under the leadership of Major Vallon, was attached—though remaining autonomous—to the battalion formerly created by Lieutenant-Colonel Gambiez. The two together constituted a light brigade, commanded by Gambiez, and designed to undertake sudden attacks.

The officers of the British unit at Staoueli and those of the French unit at Sidi-Ferruch usually met in the evenings in Algiers. Lionel had often met Colonel Gambiez and Major Vallon. Vallon, a brilliant and energetic man, was one of my friends at the Science Polytechnique, and was immersed as I was in the study of economics.

Colonel Gambiez, an enterprising professional soldier, had a few months earlier led the successful operations in Corsica and on Elba. Lionel admired both of them, and they both noted the courage and leadership qualities of the young British captain. They realised that Lionel would have much to offer the units training at Sidi-Ferruch if he were willing to avail them of his expertise in parachute techniques and guerrilla warfare he had acquired in Yugoslavia.

Among these brilliant officers and young men brimming with enthusiasm and generosity, Lionel rediscovered the French atmosphere he had so much enjoyed in 1939-40. He conceived the idea of joining the French army in order to finish the campaign alongside his fellow Frenchmen. He made his application simultaneously to both the French and British commands. This idea had occurred to him before. As early as 1 January 1944, when he was finishing his parachute training in Palestine, he had made similar enquiries with the French Liaison Officer attached to the French consulate in Jerusalem, specifying that he would hope to join a parachute or a commando unit in the future. His request was not granted, but this time he was more successful. In a letter of 29 July 1944, the British colonel gave him permission to serve in the French commando unit on loan, and if necessary to go on operations, while he waited for official approval to join the French army.

During this waiting period, Lionel still wore his British officer's uniform while working as an instructor in the French training facility at Sidi-Ferruch. He supervised the building of a magnificent training pitch, complete with all possible obstacles: walls, ditches, rivers, barbed wire and so on. His physical endurance won the admiration of all his students. Every day, he led three teams through the training course, each of which was exhausted by the end of their turn, while after his three circuits he was still as fresh as a daisy. He gave his students more than simply technical training: he added rules of conduct that were to be obeyed as proper orders. The first of these rules is still imprinted on the minds of his trainees: 'You are not to die for your country; it is the enemy who must die for it.'

Lionel's admission into the French army raised administrative difficulties. He had never served in the French army, and the rules were that one should join as a private. He said he did not mind in the least, and would serve as a private if he could not be taken on as an officer.

The French hierarchy was however reluctant to apply the letter of the law to the young captain who had served in the Balkans and had a chestful of British medals. In the end, Major Vallon put in a request to the Minister for War, Mr Diethelm, who decreed that in these exceptional circumstances the British captain could be appointed second lieutenant in the 1st French Commandos.

It was a great day for Lionel; he hoped to go off on operations immediately. However, his patience was to be tested yet again.

There were insufficient boats to transport the unit. A cruiser, the Montcalm, finally arrived. The young men, who were very anxious to join the fighting, declared that it was not to leave without them. The captain was not keen to take on this task, which was outside his normal duties. He gave many good reasons: he had insufficient provisions and a propeller in need of repair. Nothing would dissuade the troops, who boarded during the night and left Algiers on 9 October, commanded by Major de Foucaucourt, standing in for Major Vallon who had gone on ahead.

The unit disembarked at Toulon on the 10th, and after stopping in Marseille was sent on to the little town of Beure, four kilometres from Besançon. Beure was to be their centre of operations, from where detachments of different sizes were to go out on various attack missions, and where they were to regroup afterwards for rest and recuperation. As we shall see, circumstances dictated there were few, and only brief, periods of rest. I decided I would go on a pilgrimage, following the last few weeks of Lionel's life from Beure to Masevaux.

Beure is a charming village, clinging to the sunny side of a rocky hill. Lionel reached it on 23 October and was sent with his adjutant to the dairywoman, Mme Mougin, a welcoming and quiet lady with grey hair who had very fond memories of the young man billeted on her. When she first saw him arrive, tanned, his dark hair unruly, she was wary of his demanding and fierce manner. But she came to see him quite differently.

It seems he made himself thoroughly at home, including in his untidy room. He helped himself to fruit when hungry, warmed himself in front of the stove after a long march, his athletic body naked to the waist without particular pride. He took over a table and wrote for hours, but he had the grace to offer a little gift to his hostess in generous compensation. When he had finished work, he liked to chat with Mme Mougin of all the things he had on his heart: his mother, his brothers, his past and his future, and she discovered him to be the generous, loyal, good and gentleman he was.

The winter started harshly, and his men were cold. One day, he arrived at the dairy with a huge parcel. 'Look, Mme Mougin, I'm happy today. You told me it was not possible to find any woollen clothes in Besançon. I went to see the president of the hosiers' guild, and thanks to him I have been able to provide a woollen cardigan and two pairs of socks for each of my men. It's a good day.'

Lionel made some good friends among his fellow soldiers, especially Lieutenant Saint-Mleux. He ate every meal with them in their camp kitchen, placed under a trellis in a charming spot against the rocky hillside. It was the Auberge du Bout du Monde.[75] Not that the mess dinners lasted very long. Lionel did not smoke, drink or play games, and as soon as the meal

was over he would go to his men's billet. Every day ended with
this last but not least important duty. With careful attention
to detail he required his group to do their utmost and to do it
well. Everything had to be ready for the next day, and all orders
given. Nothing was left to chance, not even the evening menu.
Lionel wanted to ensure that his men ate well, and the standard
rations were on occasion extended with a few extra items paid
for by the canteen's petty cash, which owed its funds, in large
part, to the lieutenant's pay packet.

Once all the duties had been seen to, Lionel liked to chat
with his men before leaving them. Sergeant Trompette told
me the formula for this more relaxed hour: Lionel would
drop the tone of command, and the conversation would turn
to general enquires of his men—though not in a formal sense
of questioning or with any false affectation—to which they
replied as fully as they chose, with respect. They would refer
to him as 'the captain' or 'the lieutenant'. He would ask about
each man's past life and plans for the future. In his platoon, a
number of the mechanics said they were worried they would
not easily find work after the war. Lionel discussed with them
a plan to build up a network of good garages along the major
main roads of the country, and offered to back the project.

Sometimes, the men asked him questions, wanting to know
more about the somewhat mysterious adventures of their
commanding officer since the outbreak of war. Lionel was
discreet, but picked out a few stories that interested them, or
made them laugh. One day, the platoon he was leading was
on guard duty at Buckingham Palace. As is the custom, the
King and Queen invited him to a small lunch party. The men
were bursting with curiosity, 'What did the King say? And the

[75] World's End Inn.

Queen? Did you tell them you were French?' To which he replied, 'I was very careful not to. Just think! A French soldier guarding the King of England—the London newspapers would have had a field day!'

They also discussed the atrocities he had seen committed by the Germans. He never tired of this subject, and his hate was bottomless. He had killed boches, and would kill more. He not only hated the Germans, he despised them. He pulled from a pocket the four or five louis that he was carefully guarding in order to bribe a German sentry if ever he was made prisoner. If he were killed, the louis were to be paid into the canteen petty cash, and his revolver, watch and personal objects were to be distributed between his subordinate officers and his men. If he fell, though, his strict orders were that the men should continue fighting under the orders of the next most senior officer, who would find in his left pocket the current marching orders. He was in any case confident that, as in Yugoslavia, he would continue to dodge the bullets.

These conversations were subject to neither hierarchy nor protocol, and Lionel was generally in a good mood. Only one thing irritated him – carping criticism of the attitude of British and American troops or of the effectiveness of their military actions. 'It's really silly to denigrate our allies. I have better reason than anyone to know, as I have been to America, I have served for four years in the British army, and I was not born French. So I have neither pride nor prejudice. Why not simply thank them? Do you know Tacitus's assertion that "Kindness is welcome to the extent the debt can be repaid. When it goes too far gratitude turns into hatred"? Well, if any country may express gratitude without humiliation, it is France, since

she has returned the favour in advance, having fought for
years for the freedom of other countries—the United States,
Italy, Greece, Belgium, Poland—and she will no doubt have
opportunity in the future to do the same again. France was
defeated in 1870, and yet recovered sufficiently to stop the
flood of German imperialism at the Marne in 1914, for the
benefit of the whole world.'

The time would come to stop chatting, and the men would
stand and salute: 'Good night, captain.'

During those few days in Beure, it was hard to hold back
the young men who were keen to reach the front line and face
the enemy.

**

They did not have long to wait. On 1 November, the unit
moved off for its first operation. Mme Mougin bade farewell to
Lionel, who glowed with enthusiasm.

They were transported by lorry to Saint-Amé, near
Remiremont, and on 3 November they attacked an important
vantage point, Le Haut du Tôt. Their detachment was due to
be relieved by infantry units with tanks and artillery. These
failed to turn up, so the detachment was to hold the position
they had gained two days previously. About half the men were
killed.

Lionel was given his first French army decoration, and
was grateful to return to the neat, sun-drenched little house
in Beure where he was warmly welcomed. He felt the job had
been well done, but grieved the heavy losses which could have
been avoided had the commandos been reinforced earlier. It
was a short respite. Eight days later, Lionel informed Mme

Mougin that they were to leave that evening for a series of important operations in the direction of Belfort and Upper Alsace. He spent the morning packing his tin trunk, and then asked for a little wooden chest, in which he put his treasured personal possessions: letters from his mother, his British medals and a few items of clothing. He nailed it shut and asked Mme Mougin—it seems he had some kind of premonition—to send the box to his mother if he did not return. Then he went to have a rest in his room. Mme Mougin knocked on his door when it was time to leave, and he was not in a cheerful mood: 'What crime have I committed to have to live like this?' Then he pulled himself together and turned to his adjutant, who shared the room: 'Come on, let's go.' At the door, he stopped and asked Mme Mougin if he could kiss her on both cheeks, and then he quickly jumped into the lorry, and they set off.

After some minor operations at Semondans, Trémoins, Couthenans, Chagey, Châlonvillars, the unit was given an important and difficult order: they were to find the weak point in the defences around Belfort.

Major de Foucaucourt was ordered to take the village of Essert by night, by going through a tunnel under the canal that served the enemy as a moat, easily defended. The attack happened on 20 November at 2 a.m. The men had to negotiate low-lying ground, cross an anti-tank ditch six metres deep and barbed-wire defences. The surprise attack was a complete success. There were significant losses among the commandos, but German losses were heavier. Belfort was freed by the end of the day. What was left of the unit was taken by lorry towards Giromagny, which was taken on the 23rd, and then sent on a forced march under torrential freezing rain to attack the

Gestapo headquarters at Saint-Nicolas, near Rougemont-le-Château. In spite of their efforts, they only reached the village just after the Germans had left it. On the 24th, Lionel led two successful patrol expeditions.

On 25 November, the unit headquarters received orders to take Masevaux, by surprise if possible. Masevaux was defended by 1,200 Germans supported by mortar batteries on the hills to the north of the village. The commandos crossed a mountain and gained sight of the town. The Germans had blown up the three bridges over the river Doller and had retreated to the more populated northern bank. Major Foucaucourt divided his men into three units, each one charged with crossing the river using the rubble of a destroyed bridge, and establishing a bridgehead on the other side while waiting for heavier forces to arrive.

Major Foucaucourt, Captain Ruais and Lionel were all in the centre unit.

Lionel led the way with his loyal companion-in-arms, Sergeant Trompette, who had been with him from the start of operations. At 5.30 p.m. it was already dark. Lionel put down his kitbag, crossed the river cautiously and started along a little street about fifty metres long that led from the riverside to the town hall square, a large space with a charming fountain in the centre.

A shadow seemed to emerge from the wall on his left: a German sentry. He was a big lad, and before he had time to shoot, Lionel fell on him, disarmed him and engaged him in hand-to-hand combat. In a few seconds he had thrown him to the ground, and knelt to put his knife in. As he was about to finish him off, the German made a desperate movement so that the knife cut open his stomach. He started yelling and calling for help. In that tragic moment, Trompette held his gun pointing at the German's temple. He said to Lionel, 'Let me finish him off.' Lionel answered, 'No, he's mine.' He gave a few more blows with the knife, and then left him moaning. He then turned to the Alsatian guide, Prax Martin, and asked the way to the station and set off towards it. But the sentry's yells had alerted the enemy. During the minute or two they had been fighting, a German car armed with a machine-gun had arrived. At the very moment when Lionel came out onto the square, he was shot point-blank with a full round in the chest and head. He died instantly and fell in front of the chemist's shop on the corner. German reinforcements arrived, and the commandos had a very tough fight on their hands. It took several hours of intense shooting to establish the occupation of the street from the bridge to the square. On the following day, an infantry battalion known as the 'bataillon de Gaillardon' came to reinforce the commando unit. Within twenty-four hours, and at the cost of many lives, the town of Masevaux was fully liberated. The commando unit had now lost about 75% of its men.

When Lionel fell, his comrades laid his body along the wall by the chemist's shop. Later that night, two Alsatians carried him into the ground floor of a neighbouring house. All those who had fallen in that area were gathered together the following day and the carpenter, Enderling, came with a team of men with biers to bury them. They had to cross the square, still raked by enemy machine-gun fire. The procession moved along protected by a line of German prisoners. The shooting stopped and an hour later, the coffins were carried back across the square to the small flower-laden cemetery. There, side by side, without distinction of rank or religion, lie the bodies of the first Frenchmen to die liberating the first town in Upper Alsace.

Appendix

'Lionel Mosséri', by Lieutenant-Colonel Vallon, Deputy Director of General de Gaulle's Cabinet, and formerly of the First Unit of Commandos de France.

18 December, 1945

In the spring of 1944 a young British captain visited me at Sidi-Ferruch. He told me he was French and wanted to serve in the French commandos that Henri Astier and I were gathering and training on African soil in preparation for the imminent landings in France. He was called Lionel Mosséri and he was twenty-two years old.

The War Minister agreed, that as an exceptional favour, he should be appointed second lieutenant in the French army, given that he had already, in three years, reached the rank of captain through his participation in the hard battles of the British commandos in Yugoslavia and Italy.

The 'Commandos de France' recruited young men, mostly aged between eighteen and twenty-one, who had escaped from France in order to serve in the army to liberate their homeland. They had all volunteered for the demanding and disciplined duties required of specialist troops, and to train as parachutists. Lionel Mosséri, who fitted in very happily with them, was put in charge of the section protecting the unit headquarters. His self-confidence, his dedication and his kindness very quickly gained him the friendship of all those he worked with.

He could be both solemn and light-hearted; serious and full of flights of fancy. He took excellent care of his men, of their food, their housing and their instruction; of their morale and of their appearance, so that his Protection Section became a model small unit.

At the beginning of November 1944, in our first engagements in the Vosges before Gérardmer, Lionel Mosséri gave himself heart and soul to the fighting, showing the same tireless bravery as his men.

On the evening of 6 November, our unit withdrew from a victorious skirmish, leaving a considerable number of dead, but strengthened by the sense of having proved itself and demonstrated both to the enemy and to our companions-in-arms that the French commandos, although not specifically trained to fight as infantry on a continuous front, were both brave and effective.

A few days later—on 18, 19 and 20 November—the French commandos were sent to attack Belfort. During a night-time assault on the village of Essert, Lionel Mosséri and his unit once again demonstrated their military brilliance. After the occupation of Belfort, the commandos were transported by lorry to Giromagny. From there they were given an extremely hazardous mission, together with other shock troop units, under the command of Lieutenant-Colonel Gambiez: they were to move through the Vosges forests and penetrate enemy lines at the points of lowest surveillance. The first French commando unit moved more than seven kilometres behind the German line and, on the night of 25 November, seized the little Alsatian town of Masevaux. It was a surprise attack, and succeeded in spite of fierce resistance from the Germans. It was on that evening that Lionel Mosséri, having just fatally stabbed an enemy sentry, was killed by a point-blank round of machine-gun fire. He was buried the following day with some of our other comrades while the battle was still raging around Masevaux.

He was mentioned in dispatches and made a Chevalier de la Légion d'Honneur.

His letters, which his mother has faithfully gathered, are a fitting tribute to his many gifts of both mind and heart.

Throughout his short life he displayed both purpose and a sense of community. We shall remember him as one who was brave among the brave, and always wore the smile of those who had hopes for the future.

Louis Vallon.

Lieutenant-Colonel Vallon

Formerly commanding officer of the

First Unit of the Commandos de France.

Letter from Colonel Gambiez, officer commanding the shock-troop regiment which included the First Unit of the Commandos de France.

Shock-Troop Regiment, Airborne Infantry
SP. 70,936, 5 December, 1945

Colonel Gambiez Commanding Officer,
Shock-Troop Regiment, Airborne Infantry
to
Mme R. L. Marlio, 8, rue Guy-de-Maupassant, Paris 16ième.

Madame,

I knew your son Lionel extremely well, and thought of him as a younger brother. I was very fond of him for his high ideals, his burning faith, his unusual energy and his very wide cultural interests. He was like a cherished child, and we entrusted to his care a valuable unit—all hand-picked, first-class men.

You can therefore imagine the great sorrow we felt when he died such a heroic death at Masevaux. He was very specially ours, and with him, we lost a small part of ourselves, of the spirit of the unit.

Madame, please accept my most respectful condolences.

1st Airborne Regiment,

Colonel Gambiez.

Letter from Lieutenant Saint-Mleux, friend of Lionel
Mosséri and fellow soldier.

8 March, 1945

Madame,

You suffered a cruel loss several months ago. Since that
time we have continued to fight. We are now, thanks to his
sacrifice and that of many others, able to guard a border along
the Rhine and enjoy some respite. So I would now like to offer
you my most respectful and sincere condolences, and tell you
some of my memories of Lionel.

Your son and I were very close friends. We were both very
young. We were part of the same mess, and shared not only a
part-English heritage but also our intellectual life. During the
three weeks in Algiers before we embarked, we lived in the same
tent, in a British camp to which we had been invited because of
our English roots. I have the most treasured memories of our
life together, during which we formed a deep bond.

Then we left, and it was Lionel's dearest wish to do so.
He had chosen this particularly vulnerable unit clearly aware
of the danger, and determined to give his best. We were all
particularly impressed by his valiant willingness to give up his
rank as captain in the British army and to embrace a much
lower rank as second lieutenant in the French commandos.

What can I say of his bravery, other than that it was of the
highest calibre? You know that at Masevaux on 25 November
he fell at the head of the front line of those who led the
liberation of the first Alsatian town in the southern Vosges
district. He fell without a word, hit by a burst of machine-gun
fire to the chest.

Madame, I know how great your grief must be. I just wanted to assure you that we, I and his fellow soldiers, share it with you, and we hope this might soften your grief. We all treasure the memory of a man we loved much.

Next month, I hope that we may meet and that I may perhaps be able to give you any details you would particularly wish to hear. Please be assured that I am ready at your bidding. In the meantime may I offer my sincere and respectful condolences.

A. Saint-Mleux.

Memories of Lionel Mosséri from Mr Philip Newell, former headmaster of Gresham's School.

Lionel came to Gresham's School, near the coast of Norfolk in England, when he was already a big, strong boy. We both arrived within the same year at this school, which is nearly four hundred years old. I was the new headmaster and he was a pupil who came from a milieu very different to that of his fellow pupils. It would be a challenge for both of us to adapt to this community.

This British school has a great respect for individuals and, insofar as is possible, given the gregarious instincts of youngsters, it has a tradition of great tolerance towards those who stand out from the crowd in terms of their ideas and their habits. Lionel was different. With characteristic instinct, he wanted to preserve and defend—sometimes even emphasise—the difference. He could exasperate the most patient: he always relished a fight, keen to drill down to the fundamental issues of every matter.

We often talked together. I defended the authority and the methods used by the school (which did not use corporal punishment) while he would advocate a particular break with established tradition, or try to justify something subversive he had said or done. We often talked both at length and in depth, and got to know each other well. I was delighted when he became a good defender on the football pitch, especially since he had at first decided he would never learn, and then that he could and would learn.

There was a time when he was not convinced that school learning was of use to him. However, he then found himself being taught by Donald Greatwood, one of the masters at the school. Mr Greatwood taught him French, and his enthusiasm sparked ambition in Lionel. As a result, he did extremely well both in the exams he took in England and in those he took at home in Paris.

My wife and I knew him intimately by the time he finished school, but it was his brief visits during his periods of leave from the army that enabled us to see his character flourish.

He returned to England from America in order to join the fighting, and he was always wanting to see action. The long wait he had to endure, as an ordinary soldier and operating well below his intellectual capabilities, must have been particularly trying to such a keen and impatient person. It was a great joy to us to see how well he reacted, and, starved of suitable intellectual activities, rented a room, gathered some books together and gave himself to preparing for his life's work.

When he was promoted as an officer in the KRRC, an old and excellent regiment, he was justly proud, and we were even more so. My happiest memories of Lionel are from this time.

He had a few days' leave close to Christmas, so he came to stay, and shared in our homely preparations. I can see him now, sitting in the nursery one evening, with a paintbrush in each hand, helping to finish off toys that were to be sent to Plymouth and on to households that had lost their homes. He was completely absorbed, not only in a task he was finding challenging, but also in the discussion we were having on Walter Lippmann's The Good Society. He used the paintbrush like a baton to emphasise his points of view as he asked deeply searching questions in a bid to expose our deepest thoughts. I shall always treasure this memory: his analytical mind, and the thirst for knowledge that had been present in the child and had flourished in the gifted and delicately courteous man.

Letter from Lady Halifax, wife of the British Ambassador in Washington, British Embassy, Washington, DC.

11 January, 1945

Dear Mme Marlio,

I hope you will forgive me for writing to you.

We are full of grief for you both in your great loss. May we please share in the pride and the admiration felt by all for such a brave and splendid soldier, who died so nobly for his country and for the Allied cause, after such a wonderful service record.

....

In deepest sympathy, yours sincerely,

Dorothy Halifax.

Letter from André Maurois, author and soldier in the
Free French Forces

13 January, 1945

My dear friends,

My wife and I were terribly sad to learn of the death of your
son. We know what he meant to you, and his heroism must
make you love him all the more. His military life could not have
been more honourable, and I know of few more distinguished
service records, in such a short span of time. He made it to
captain in three years, and then voluntarily dropped to second
lieutenant in order to join the French army. As a parachutist he
braved many dangers, and then moved into the commandos.
His is a career both moving and extraordinary. His sacrifice
was most noble, but your grief will not be lessened by this.
Please accept our deepest and fondest sympathy.

André Maurois.

Letter from Mlle Reine Braun

3 February, 1945

My very dear friends,

... Lionel was in some way our child, a kind of superior
Marc,[76] a luminous person whom we admired and who
delighted us. We rejoiced at every one of his achievements as
much as if he had been our very own...

---

[76] The name of her brother.

Citations of Lionel Mosséri, dispatches of the Commandos de
France, 1st General Dispatch, Operation at Haut-du-Tôt
Second Lieutenant Lionel Mosséri,
1st Unit of French Commandos

A young officer, who had volunteered to join the French
commandos and had commanded the Headquarters Protection
Unit, demonstrated bravery, calm under fire and ability to
command during action on 3rd to 6th November 1944 in the
area of Haut-du-Tôt and the Lyris forest.

First French Army, Certified copy
1st Shock-Troop Battalion Formation, S.P. 70,930,
14 May, 1945
3rd Shock-Troop Battalion
Squadron-Leader d'Astier de la Vigerie,
Commanding Officer, 3rd Shock-Troop Battalion

Citation of Lionel Mosséri in the Order of the Army
Decision no. 802
At the suggestion of the Minister for War, the President
of the Provisional Government of the French Republic
and Commander in Chief of the Army makes the following
mention:

Order of the Army, Posthumous citation
Lionel Mosséri, second lieutenant in the 1st Unit of
French Commandos.

An officer of great gallantry, who gave up his rank of
captain gained in the British army in order to have the honour
of serving as second lieutenant in the French commando unit.

He showed signal bravery, always in the lead, during the unit's actions between 19th and 25th November, 1944, in particular at Essert, on the 20th, in a pre-dawn operation against a strongly defended German position guarding Belfort.

On 25 November, during a daring night-time assault he forced a passage across a bridge into Masevaux and was killed at point-blank range, having felled an enemy with his dagger in fierce hand-to-hand combat.

This dispatch awards the Croix de Guerre with bar, and will be published in the Journal Officiel of the French Republic.

Paris, 10 June, 1945.

Signed: De Gaulle

Letter from Claude Mosséri to his mother on learning of his brother's death[77]

'I kill so that others will not have to do so.'

This is a quote from the last letter my brother wrote to me. It is not difficult to see what he meant. He was trying, by risking his life—and in the end by losing it—to help the world gain what had never yet been achieved: everlasting peace.

Yes, in early 1940 he joined the British army not out of a sense of revenge, but because he had seen light even in darkness. He left home four long years ago, knowing he would not return for six years at least. Yes, he gave all that up in order to get to the light he had glimpsed. And he not only wished to reach this everlasting light, but he gave all he had, and more, to do so. He volunteered for a succession of dangerous missions. This was not enough for him, so he joined the commandos. Every day he saw the light growing a little closer. Life as a commando, he

---

[77] The reader is asked to bear in mind that the writer of this letter was only fourteen years old at the time, and therefore to excuse any stylistic infelicities.

realised, would not enable him to reach that light fast enough, so he joined the parachute regiment. This he enjoyed, as there was nothing more dangerous. One might have thought he had then done his duty and more, but no. After eleven jumps he was ordered to rest for six months, but refused. The British army would not take him on anywhere else—they knew he deserved and needed a long rest. He didn't agree. The only way to continue the battle was to switch armies, so he did.

He gave up his rank as a captain to become a second lieutenant so he could continue to fight. Yes, he was now in the French army. He was among men who loathed the Germans and would have given their right arm to go and fight them. The French army was not well endowed with either military or health equipment. He was leading his men at Belfort, capturing a pivotal crossroads. He wrote: 'I am in the last hundred metres of the race, and nothing has yet happened to me.' But a month later, on 25 November, 1944, the Germans got him.

He had done much, maybe even too much, but I'm sure he died saddened that the job he had started was not yet finished. I know, however, that this is not true. I am very, very proud of him. I know he tried with all his heart to gain that everlasting light of peace for the world.

I know he died to achieve this, and for something else too: so others would not have to kill. Knowing this, I shall follow in his footsteps and do my best to bring to fruition the task he so gallantly, bravely and generously began.

Claude.

Letter from Colonel Jacobsen de Rose
French Military Government, Hesse-Rhineland Delegation
Mainz, 28 March, 1946

Madame,

I received your letter only yesterday. I am replying as soon as possible, but fear I shall not be able to give you the information you are seeking.

I knew your son Lionel Mosséri very well; I admired him deeply and worked with him on many occasions. As you know, he was a very modest man and did not speak of himself nor of his gallantry. We hardly knew much of his history, and in spite of our requests he never spoke of his earlier actions. I am very sorry to have to tell you this. All the more so since we were close friends. I owe a great deal to Lionel both in terms of technical knowledge and in terms of personal qualities. He was an example to us, his fellow soldiers, of bravery, of daring, and of moral and spiritual uprightness. His fighting at Masevaux was the stuff of legend.

Mme Marlio, you should know that I have been most moved by thus revisiting my memories of Lionel, and I must convey to you my deepest sympathy at your very cruel loss. We shall always treasure the name of Lionel Mosséri as a symbol of the highest purity and honesty. Some there are who are so pure, so completely committed to their ideal and their rule of life that they are too good for this world. We survivors can only bewail our unworthiness and try to emulate the lives of those from whose example we have learned. Please forgive this short note, in which I have only been able to record my gratitude for a loyal friendship.

Yours most faithfully,

T. Jacobsen de Rose (Colonel Jacobsen de Rose).

Sir Thomas G. Devitt, Easton Glebe, Dunmow, Essex
Madame Louis Marlio,
2940 Cortland Pl. N.W., Washington 8, D.C.

Dear Madame Marlio,

Thank you for your letter of 31 May, 1946. May I first express my deepest sympathy at the sad death of your son, Lionel Mosséri.

He was not under my command when he fell, and I knew nothing of it. Had he been under my command I would have written to you personally at the time he died to tell you of my great sadness.

Lionel joined the special service unit, called the Raiding Support Regiment, which I had raised and trained in Palestine. As far as I can remember, he was among the first group of volunteers to join our unit, in October 1943, but I had more than eighty officers who joined at various times. I therefore can't give you the exact date of his arrival, but it was either in October or November 1943. Neither do I recall the specific operations he was engaged in while in my regiment, as we were divided into sub-divisions operating everywhere over Greece, Italy and the Dalmatian islands in small units. I don't remember exactly where he was or the precise operations he took part in under my command. He left my regiment to join the A Force (I think that was the name of the unit), which was another extremely secret organisation in which he thought he would see more action than had he stayed with me. If he was engaged in action while in my regiment, it will have been over the Dalmatian coast and on the Dalmatian islands, supporting the Yugoslavs or the commandos carrying out our occupation.

I am sure he was not in Greece. It was in June 1944 that he left my regiment to join the A Force, and I was told that he took part in landings, probably by parachute, in southern France – this is very likely given his perfect knowledge of the French language and the fact that he died among the French commandos.

The Raiding Support Regiment was not a parachute troop like the Parachute Regiment, but was specially trained to undertake various missions, only one aspect of which was the descent by parachute. The regiment was part of the Middle East Raiding Forces, a kind of super-commando group.

I am most sorry that I cannot supply further details, but the operations in which he took part were free of particular incident, so they gave rise to no special reports. What I can add is that your son was an extremely charming and delightful young officer, full of promise, very thoughtful and conscientious, who thought at all times of his men and of how best to help them and train them.

It is tragic to think that such a fine and gifted young man gave his life to serve his friends and the British army. His loss will have been felt by all his friends, and all the more by his family. May I once more, dear lady, offer you my deepest sympathy and my condolences.

Thomas G. Devitt.

Location of Masevaux in France

Masevaux 1944: the final conflict

Lightning Source UK Ltd.
Milton Keynes UK
UKOW05f0945101113

220739UK00004B/9/P

9 781906 509231